THE LONDON, BRIGHTON & SOUTH COAST RAILWAY

THE BENNETT COLLECTION

'D' Class tank No. 233 *Handcross* in the easternmost platform at Brighton, having brought in a passenger working from Tunbridge Wells, No. 233 being at that time a Tunbridge Wells engine. This was a sample spare parts creation which had been sent to Neilson of Glasgow who constructed No's 234-267. They wrote to Stroudley suggesting they be incorporated in an extra engine, saving £160 on this particular locomotive. Stroudley agreed and on 5th May 1882 Neilson's Order Book read: 'One 0-4-2 tank for the Brighton Railway similar in all respects to E527. The samples received from that Company, except for the valve gear and connecting rods, to be incorporated'.

© Klaus Marx and Lightmoor Press 2011
Designed by Ian Pope
British Library Cataloguing-in-Publication Data. A catalogue record for this book is available from the British Library
ISBN 13: 978 1899889 61 7
All rights reserved. No part of this publication may be reproduced, stored in a retrieval system or transmitted in any form or by any means, electronic, mechanical, photocopying, recording or otherwise, without the written permission of the publisher.

Lightmoor Press

Lightmoor Press is an imprint of Black Dwarf Lightmoor Publications Limited
144b Lydney Industrial Estate, Harbour Road
Lydney, Gloucestershire, GL15 4EJ
Printed and bound by T J International, Padstow, Cornwall

At the peak period of Bennett's photography, Douglas Earle Marsh was introducing his Atlantic tanks, this locomotive first entering traffic in October 1907. No. 6 of Class 'I1', a classification confusing to typesetters, of Brighton shed is in charge of a late afternoon stopping train head coded for Portsmouth. Over in the sidings one of Dorking's numerous 'D' Class tanks shunts stock.

THE LONDON, BRIGHTON & SOUTH COAST RAILWAY

THE BENNETT COLLECTION

KLAUS MARX

Henry Bennett has composed an elegant portrait of 'D' Class 0-4-2T No. 269 (formerly *Crawley*) on a Brighton train passing an occupation crossing to the south of Steyning Station. The cutting behind the train is portrayed in the view on page 86. No. 269 lost its name in October 1907 so the photograph must have been taken after that date.

A special excursion to the south coast is brought down past Wivelsfield by Class 'I1' No. 4 which entered traffic in August 1907. The driver allocated was William Clarke, but in Wilfred S. Palmer's notebook this has for some reason been crossed through. Between 1925 and 1932 Maunsell decided to rebuild the class as each in turn fell due to visit Eastleigh Works becoming Class 'I1x'.

CONTENTS

INTRODUCTION

What's in a picture? Quite a lot, in fact. This album with its extended captions has sought to be explanatory, thanks to the several sources of information. In the first place the basic details written in a single sentence by Walter Bennett in his inimitable print, then Ralph Stent's pencilled comments on the reverse of many of the postcard prints I passed up to him, inviting his memories of the scene and location, and eliciting his personal memories of those far off days, now more than a century ago, and thirdly notes by John Minnis, the Brighton Circle's Photographic Steward. Other valuable sources have been the late Wilfred S. Palmer's *A Brighton Spotter's Notebook* (1900 - 1907) and with some entries up to 1910, which chiefly coincides with Bennett's main period of photography, and D. L. Bradley's *Locomotives of the LB&SCR* trilogy for some double checking.

Though a few of the photographs have been published previously elsewhere, it was felt best to show the collection at its most comprehensive and visually interesting. I am grateful to my long standing friends John Minnis for double checking the captions and for further suggestions, and to Lawrence Marshall who has identified a handful of Bennett pictures not in the main collection. My thanks must also go to my good friend, Nick Wellings, who lives in Brighton and has kindly researched the local archives and directories. Finally to Lightmoor Press for taking on the production of this worthy album.

The Bennett collection belongs to the Bluebell Archives and I have made arrangements for the royalty payments to be paid to the Bluebell Railway towards their huge expenses involved in battling through to East Grinstead, and later hopefully through Ardingly to Haywards Heath.

Klaus Marx, 2011

'E4' Class No. 482 *Newtimber* was a resident of the Horsted Keynes dump which the three musketeers first visited in 1906. Walter, the eldest of the Bennett brothers, seems to have demanded the right to be photographed most frequently. In the background is companion No. 481 *Itchingfield* which was stored there in the middle part of 1907.

Ralph Stent was the youngest of the trio and is seen on the cab steps clinging to the handrail of 'E1' Class No. 116 *Touraine*. He is wearing shorts, appropriate for the long cycle ride to Horsted Keynes, and the requisite flat cap of those days.

According to Ralph Stent, it was around 1906 that the three young musketeers started cycling to Horsted Keynes. Twenty-one year old Walter Bennett poses on the pioneer 'E3' Class radial No. 453 *Broadbridge* in the graveyard there. It had arrived on the last day of February 1907. However, it survived its eighteen months there, returning to Brighton works to re-enter traffic on 9th September 1908.

Henry and the Three Musketeers

The Bennett Collection of photographs is lodged today in the Bluebell Railway Archives. I first corresponded with Maurice Bennett when he wrote in offering items to the newly established Bluebell Museum at Sheffield Park where, as the first curator, I had set up a display in the station's Up waiting room during 1960 so that visitors to the line, following its opening on the 7th August that year, might have something of additional interest to see. In the next two years I was able to meet Maurice on a number of occasions at Sheffield Park, Haywards Heath and in his home at Jarvis Brook near Crowborough.

Initially Maurice was persuaded to loan his photographic collection of some four albums comprising 800 pictures so that the whole collection could be copied on 35mm film. I had urged this upon the late Captain Peter Manisty who gave the necessary authorisation. It proved a wise precaution because, in the end, Maurice kept three of the four albums for himself. So we have the collection on 35mm film though, unavoidably, a tiny degree of sharpness has been lost in the process. By late 1960 Maurice was seriously thinking of emigrating to Canada and of finding a good home for a part of his photographic collection which he decided to donate to the Bluebell Archives. The collection neatly covers the period from the late 1890s to well into the era of Douglas Earle Marsh (LB&SCR Locomotive Superintendent, 1905-1911) with its imposing Atlantics.

Maurice and his elder brother Walter, together with a fellow enthusiast, Ralph Stent, started photographing around 1906. The trio used their primitive bicycles at weekends to travel a fair distance to places like Horsted Keynes where locomotives awaiting works were stored during the period of the reconstruction of Brighton Works in the mid-Edwardian years. Their rural cycle rides took them to the Steyning line, up the main line as far as Haywards Heath, and to Lewes and Kemp Town to the east of Brighton.

Of particular interest was the fact that at a time when the majority of railway photographers concentrated on locomotive portraits, the Bennetts went out of their way to take trains in rural settings to scenic effect. As John Minnis, another Brighton line historian, underlines: '*Their quality was high and they also tended to compose attractive pictures showing the train in the landscape as opposed to the usual three-quarter frontal view*'.

The Bennett photographs had long been presumed to have been taken by Walter and Maurice, but one major problem was the presence of several pre-20th century photographs which could not possibly have been taken if they were only photographing at Horsted Keynes as early as 1906. These early prints were put down to the acquisition of photographs of earlier cameramen and used in the lists much as O. J. Morris offered prints of pictures taken long before he commenced photographing trains.

The breakthrough came from the back of a postcard photograph revealing the picture to be by 'H. Bennett, Cowper Street, Hove'.

PHOTO BY: H. BENNETT, COWPER ST., HOVE.

Henry Bennett was born in the middle of 1856 in Hove, the son of Benjamin, a cordwainer, and Elizabeth. Henry married Louisa Peckham (born Uckfield, 1854) in 1879. The 1881 census shows Henry to be an upholsterer living with his wife and a baby daughter at 17 West Hill Street, Brighton. By 1891 the family were living at 51 Upper North Street, Brighton with daughter Florence, now 10, having been joined by Arthur, 9, and Walter, 4. Maurice Percy was to be born later in the year. A daughter, Doris Emily, was added to the family in 1899.

1901 has the family living at 8 Blatchington Road, Hove, Henry still working on his own account as an upholsterer and with Arthur working as an electrician. By 1911 they had moved to 27 Cowper Street, Hove. Florence and Arthur were still living at home but Walter had moved to Camberwell where he was employed as a 'compressed drug maker'. Of Maurice there was no sign.

Trade directories also reveal the family business. *Kelly's Directory* for 1891 shows Henry Bennett at 51 Upper North Street as a bedding manufacturer whilst that for 1899 lists him there as an upholsterer. The 1905 edition has Henry as a furniture broker and dealer at 32 Blatchington Road. 1911 has him again as an upholsterer at 27 Cowper Street, Hove.

As well as his main business Henry was also listed in Pike's 1904 *Brighton & Hove Directory* as a dealer in photographic materials. At some point Henry appears to have turned semi-professional as a photographer taking commercial view postcards of Hove and West Blatchington. He also photographed the London, Brighton & South Coast Railway advertising the availability of their own prints to railway collectors. There are at least two lists – for 1906 and 1909 – known to be in existence advertising their products. Of his commercial view postcards a number are known but apparently nearly all have become badly faded and yellowish with age, presumably because his methods of fixing and washing photographs was defective. (Thank goodness this was not the case with his railway photographs.) The backs of the commercial cards were usually stamped in purple ink 'Photo by: H. Bennett, Cowper St., Hove.' as in the example on the previous page. Cowper Street was just round the corner from the west end of Hove railway station and was, at this time, a none too affluent area of the town.

The photographic business was obviously, therefore, run by Henry until Walter made it his particular niche (postcards were being stamped 'W. Bennett' by 1910) and it must be Henry to whom the great majority of the photographs must be attributed.

SERIES PUBLISHED BY: W. BENNETT, HOVE.

Only a dealer in photographic supplies would have had the requisite camera equipment and glass plates, and having Dad as such would explain how the sons could get hold of a camera on their rather modest means. The latter would have frequently visited Cowper Street and, with the station just round the corner, acquired their love of LB&SCR trains.

Similarly, their close and more affluent friend, Ralph Stent (christened Frederick Ralph), born towards the end of 1889, recalls how on his 13th birthday he was given a camera by his parents, who then lived at 62 Stirling Place, Hove. It was a Boots 20th Century using glass plates, and its price was 8s 9d. Ralph decided that his first picture should be of one of his favourite

This ingenious advertising card (enlarged for clarity), beautifully handwritten by young Walter Bennett (whose initials appear on the lower right-hand side of the main panel) who probably had a better education than his father, illustrates the wide following the LB&SCR had in those days. The card comes from the collection of Lawrence Marshall.

The 1909 advertising card is reproduced here at its original size. The expression FULL-SIZE PRODUCTIONS relates to the common practice of the period of contact printing a quarter plate negative onto a postcard size paper resulting in a small image set in a sea of white paper. The trains in motion section indicates that Henry Bennett was a pioneer in landscape portraits.

Even in 1909 people were prepared to spend 2d on a postcard of William Stroudley. Here Henry Bennett has topped the portrait with a choice photograph of one of his famous locomotives, 'Gladstone' Class No. 189 *Edward Blount,* Gold medal winner at the Paris Exhibition of 1889, where Stroudley was taken ill and subsequently died. The upper picture was taken at the Bennett's favourite location at Hove.

locomotives, so he went along to Brighton Station and snapped 'E4' Class No. 578 *Horsebridge*.

Ralph, who adopted a clerical career, later lived at 43 Lorna Road in a house which backed on to the coast line close to Hove Station. He kept an eagle eye on all train movements, rarely missing any locomotive working of interest that went past, and many were his vivid recollections in the pre-Grouping era. He continued there after his parents died, observing his beloved Brighton engines on into Southern Railway and BR days right to the end of Central Section steam.

After Maurice Bennett had visited the author at Sheffield Park, the latter was able to put him back in touch with Ralph Stent. On the 3rd April 1960 Ralph wrote:

> 'Yesterday afternoon and evening Maurice Bennett was here – an extremely delightful reunion after what we agreed was some fifty years since we last went out together. *Inter alia* he brought with him the box of Terrier photos, but they did not make my mouth water as I have 95% of them myself, many of which we remembered the occasion on which we originally took them. Bennett and I enjoyed our own company last night, rather than listening to O. J. Morris blather – he is so junior to us and much of what he says is not from his own experience'. [OJM was down at Brighton to show a selection of his photographs to a Railway Correspondence & Travel Society meeting].

Ralph Stent built up his own collection of photographs and in August 1971, shortly before he died, he presented it to Brighton Library for its reference section. He was intending to write a handbook as a guide to the various photographs. He said at the time: '*Although I say so, it is a most unique collection, reflecting the many happy hours of the past*'. It contained 2,402 photographs, some with their glass negatives, classified as follows: 2,195 of locomotives and trains, 168 of trams and buses, 13 of paddle steamers and 26 of vanished people and places, many never published previously. Sadly he passed away peacefully on the 11th July 1972.

Within the Bennett family collection the question arises as to which pictures were taken by whom. The conclusion must be that by far the largest quantity were taken by Henry, though the considerable number taken of the dump at Horsted Keynes were taken by the musketeers. Their negatives were obviously pooled in the interest of their entrepreneurial business. Many of the negatives were acquired by the late John Smith (now with the Lens of Sutton Association) and others by Real Photographs. The glass plates are with Rail Archive Stephenson.

No. 38 *Millwall*, built in May 1878, was a Bognor engine until the turn of the century when it was moved for a spell at Midhurst. It was transferred to the Duplicate List in December 1900, becoming No. 638. It was then sidetracked to the role of pumping engine as a stationary boiler, first at Epsom and later at Three Bridges, replacing the old Craven 0-6-0 No. 614 in July 1901 (see page 30). In October 1905 it was itself towed away to shops, evading scrap. Fitted with new cylinders and firebox and carrying wooden number plates with LOCO DEPT on its side tanks and in black livery with red lining, it served as Works pilot until 1918.

Another leading question is that of access to railway property, in particular Brighton works. It would appear that restrictions were fairly lax, judging by other contemporary railway enthusiasts like Wilfred Palmer, who managed to copy valuable details from every ex-works locomotive into his Spotter's Notebook between 1900 and 1910, exactly contemporary with the Bennett enterprise. As he described Brighton locospotting: '*There was so much more to collect than there is for the boys nowadays. For each engine there was a number, name, building date and maker, shed, driver and mileage – all (thanks to Stroudley) displayed ready to copy into our notebooks*'. All this information, including loss of engine name under the Marsh regime, are of immeasurable help in cases where the exact date of a photograph is not known, at the least to narrow down the year or even the month in which Bennett took it.

A simpler explanation could be that Walter became an employee at Brighton works – certainly he looks the part as he poses seated on the running plate of grimy locomotives under repair. The family certainly had an entreé to the works and many friends who worked there, which may account for Maurice later acquiring the works plate of Class 'I3' No. 86 which he presented to the Bluebell Railway and today reposes in the museum at Sheffield Park.

Another possible explanation is that Henry Bennett was well enough known as a railway photographer, that the works people were only too pleased to have their pictures taken, and that he had the virtual freedom of the place. It is also possible that he might have applied and been granted a free pass to railway premises if there was such a thing, though with Frank Burtt in the saddle as the official Brighton photographer, there would not have been any such requirement by the Company.

Two choices were open to me as to layout of this volume – by locomotive classes or topographically by lines. The latter appealed in that it led to a greater variety of pictures featuring different locomotives. As to the photographic locations, the majority would have been out of financial reach of the three musketeers, but Henry Bennett would have used the LB&SCR to travel on business up to London. The variety of locations represents a very wide spread across the Brighton system. It is possible that the family had acquaintances in Dorking, judging by the quite intensive photographic coverage in that area, with trips to Leatherhead, Ashtead and Epsom. Eastbourne seems particularly well covered, and Bennett could have taken his young family out for a day at the seaside, leaving them in his wife's care while he remained at the station and shed area, obtaining some rich pickings. As for the Brighton main line, Henry would have alighted at selected stations, taken his pictures and then caught the next service to Brighton or Hove.

The reader will have noted quite a number of gaps in Bennett's coverage of the system – Bognor, Littlehampton and Newhaven,

Both this and the previous photograph show teenaged Walter Bennett, taken by his father whom he may have accompanied round the works on many occasions. The year is 1908 as the latest class of locomotive, Marsh's new 'I3' Class Atlantic tanks emerged from the Erecting Shop for its trial trip (see headcode). This is No. 22 which entered traffic that March in works grey and was later fully lined out in black and white to pose for an official photograph on the Crumbles siding. The livery was retained for five months before being replaced by the standard umber. It took part in running trials mentioned by Bradley. Meanwhile the superheaters ordered by Marsh arrived and no further saturated 'I3's were built after this. Nevertheless, No. 22 survived until May 1951, only a year before this superb class became extinct.

It has been suggested that Maurice Bennett at some point in his teens was taken on at Brighton works. He seems very much at home posing here on the running plate of 'E1' Class No. 132 *Epernay*, a New Cross engine which was in works in April 1908 when at this point it lost its name to Douglas Marsh's economies. A new smokebox door appears to have been fitted as it has no hinge straps fitted as yet, being held in place by the smokebox dart.

to name some, but one needs to bear in mind that his clientele comprised railway enthusiasts, the great majority of whom were locomotive orientated, and his annual lists reflected this. Many, even in quite recent times, were seeking to collect a photograph of every LB&SC locomotive, a form of loco-spotting once removed! Bennett went where the locomotives could be seen in plenty – the Brighton main line, Lewes, Eastbourne and, of course, Horsted Keynes where up to thirty static engines stored out in the open could be picked off at leisure, as well as being a last chance saloon for veterans that would never turn a wheel again. And Bennett was quickly off the mark to photograph the latest class of locomotive or some dramatic incident.

Unfortunately, although the postcard size card photographs give the name of the locomotive and the briefest mention of the location, they omit to give the date. The only other information on the back is the date of printing e.g. 7 4 9 (7th April 1909) or 3 4 10 (3rd April 1910), which at least tells us the picture was taken before that date. The Brighton works pictures have print dates in the first three months of 1909 and in April 1910. The stretch from Haywards Heath to Hove were printed on 2nd February 1909, the Lewes pictures on 7th April 1909, the coast line astride Hove on 2nd February 1910. Ralph Stent was confused, assuming this to be the date of the photograph, but it does not wash. Henry Bennett could not possibly have been in five far flung corners of the system on the same day! All this, as the captions will show, made for some real detective research.

The Great War might have brought this enterprise to a premature end, for Maurice eased off to follow other interests, only returning to railways when preservation appeared in the form of the Bluebell Railway. But at some point, earlier rather than later, the precocious Walter Bennett took ownership of the railway photographic business, printing the sepia tinted photographs, purple-stamped on the reverse SERIES PUBLISHED BY: W BENNETT, HOVE. or in other formats. His calligraphic skills with artistic extended tails to the S, W, B, and H., were put to good use in his printed lists. Many of the pictures would have been his fathers in addition to his own. Many found their way into the Richardson Collection, a number of which are in Lawrence Marshall's collection today.

Henry was probably more interested in the furniture side of his business. He seems to have survived the war and by 1925 was living at 190 Church Road, Hove, and described in local directories as a second hand furniture dealer. He died in 1928 by which time both his sons had moved away from Hove.

In the early 1930s Walter joined the nascent Stephenson Locomotive Society which was pioneered by Brighton devotees, and taking every opportunity the Society offered for shed visits. I hold an album of Walter's in which he portrays, again in sepia prints, an example of every class of locomotive inherited or built by the London Midland & Scottish Railway, and these continued in the same sharp focused vein he registered in his Brighton days. The latest photograph in that album, which implies that he must have gravitated into LMS territory, is dated 17th September 1949, indicating that he was still photographically active into his sixties.

In the captioning of the selected photographs illustrated in this album, I have been greatly helped by the third of the musketeers, the late Ralph Stent. After Maurice had left for Canada, I took the opportunity to visit Ralph, then in his seventies and absolutely elated by the arrival on the scene of the Bluebell Railway

Marsh 'I3' Class No. 24 stands with the coaches of the Southern Belle at Lovers Walk outside Brighton in 1910. The reverse of this printed postcard has the H. Bennett stamp as reproduced on page 7 showing who was at first in charge of the photographic enterprise. No. 24 entered traffic in March 1909.

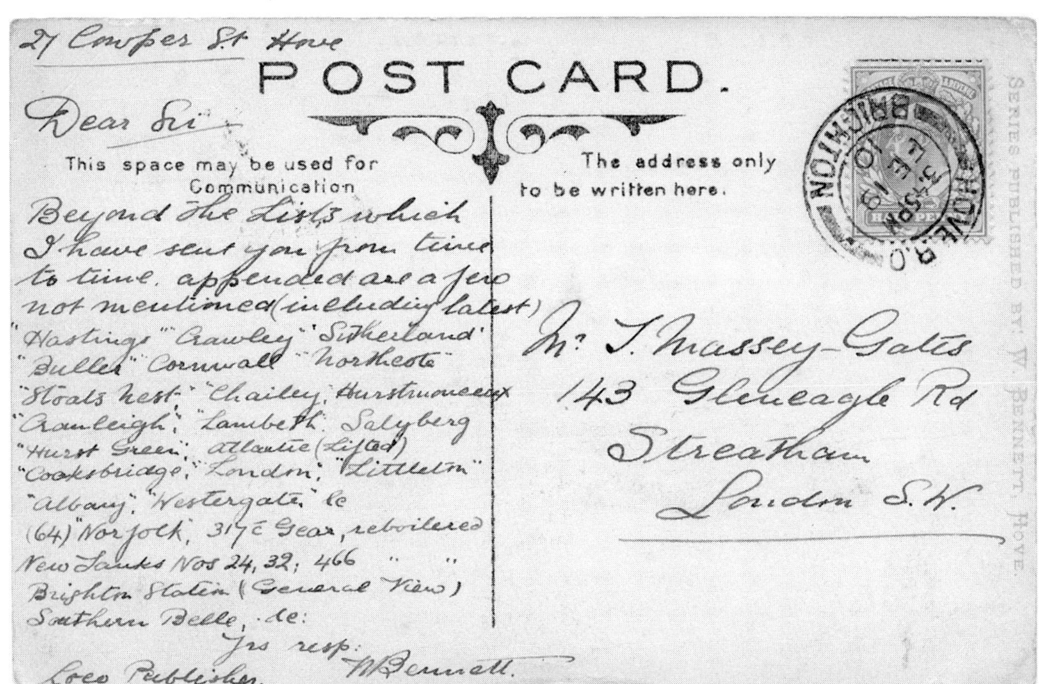
27 Cowper St Hove

POST CARD.

Dear Sir

This space may be used for Communication

The address only to be written here.

Beyond the lists which I have sent you from time to time, appended are a few not mentioned (including latest) "Hastings" "Crawley" "Sutherland" "Buller" "Cornwall" "Northcote" "Stoats Nest" "Chailey" Hurstmonceux "Crowleigh" "Lambeth" "Salzberg" "Hurst Green" Atlantic (Lifted) "Cooksbridge" "London" "Littleton" "Albany" "Westergate" &c (64) "Norfolk" 317 c Gear, reboilered New Tanks Nos 24, 32; 466 " " Brighton Station (General View) Southern Belle, &c:

Yrs resp:
W Bennett.
Loco Publisher.

Mr T. Massey-Gates
143 Gleneagle Rd
Streatham
London S.W.

SERIES PUBLISHED BY: W. BENNETT, HOVE.

This is the reverse of an identical card as that seen opposite and posted in 1910. It carries a message written by Walter together with the stamp: 'Series published by W. Bennett, Hove'.

preserving some of his old Brighton favourites. I loaned him the Bennett photographs and he kindly wrote up in pencil on the back details and memories of the scene and location. He would remark in several instances that he had taken the same photograph only a few yards further down the lineside.

No 82 "BOXHILL" — AT HOLLAND HALL. (TRIAL trip)

An example of Walter's exotic script with his 'L's looking like '7's as used in a card description.

Ralph Stent hands over his collection of photographs and his Boots 20th Century camera, using glass plates, a birthday present from his parents. Receiving the material on behalf of Brighton Library is Miss Elaine Baird, the Reference Librarian there.

Maurice Bennett specially visited Sheffield Park in 1960 to present the large works plate of 'I3' Class No. 86 to the Bluebell Railway Museum, probably an indication of some connection with Brighton works, even as late as October 1951 when this 'I3' was withdrawn.

Plate 1 : **A pair of 'B2' Class 4-4-0s prepare to leave London Bridge Station for the coast c1902. The pilot engine is No. 316 *Goldsmid* which took the name of a Brighton director and benefactor from the more humble 'D3' 0-4-4T No. 363. However, the latter had the last laugh by outliving the 'B2' by 18 years and earning a lasting niche in Brighton history by being selected to appear carrying its original name on the cap badge of every LB&SC engineman. Note the distant signals carrying the platform number to which they refer. These were used to indicate if there was a clear run to the buffer stops at the end of the platforms or whether stock was stabled there. This was important as the driver had to control his braking running into a terminus with great precision. The signal lamps are also detached from the arms which was LB&SCR practice in the 1890s.**

Plate 2 : **'D' Class tank No. 15 *Brompton* waits its next turn of duty in the shadow of the huge water tank at the side of the approaches to London Bridge Station. The vast metal tank is supported by a brick built under-floor with various rooms for pumping machinery and attendant staff. No. 15 was a Battersea engine and most likely involved in working the South London line services between London Bridge and Victoria.**

Plate 3 : **This atmospheric photograph shows how cramped was the situation at New Cross with locomotives in every corner of the complex. On the left in the process of coaling is 'G' Class Single No. 347 *Dallington*, while outside the Middle shed stands a 'D' Class 0-4-2T, No. 7 *Bermondsey*, also of New Cross with another Single behind.**

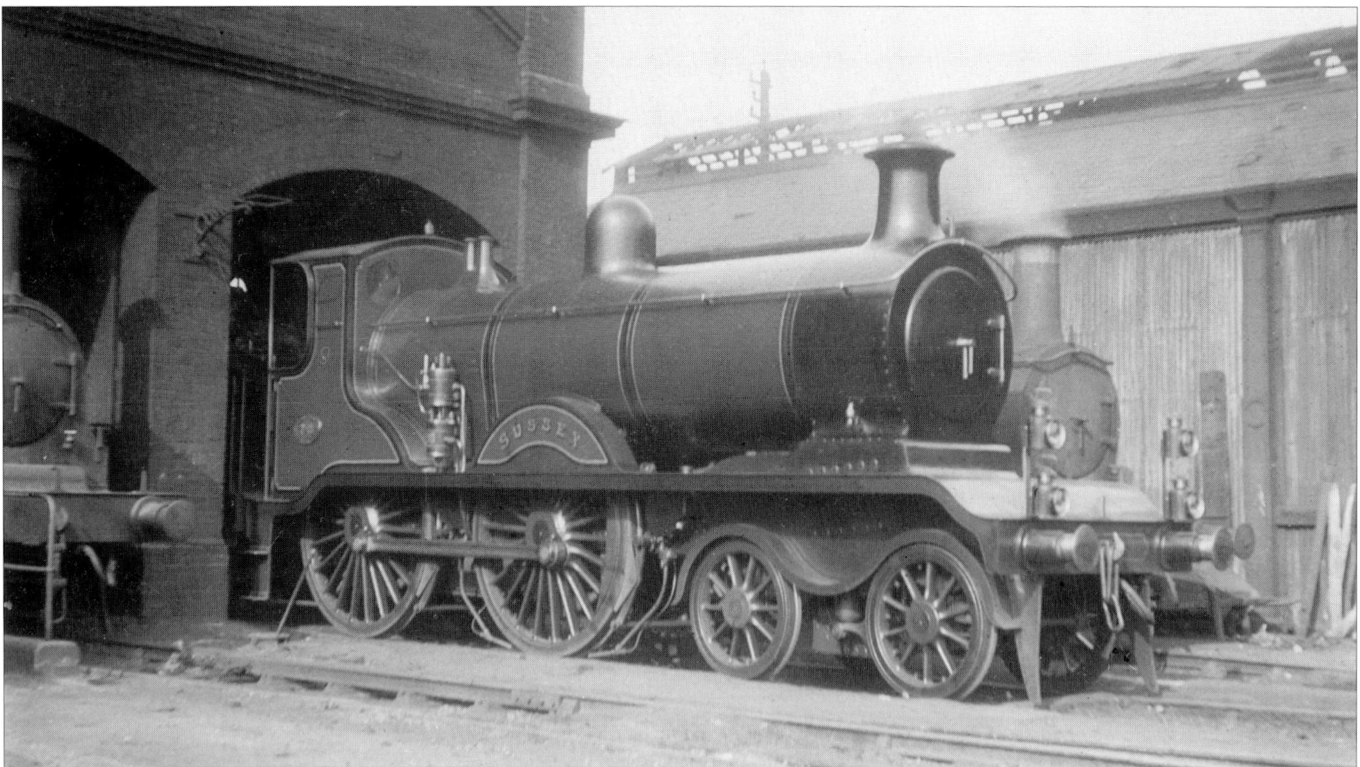

Plate 4 : **'B4' Class No. 72 *Sussex* peeps out of the Middle Shed at New Cross. The Company's home county name was bandied around several members of the class. It lost its name in July 1907 when it succumbed to the Marsh umber livery, but in September 1908 the name was conferred upon the pioneer 'B4' No. 52, replacing *Siemens*, one of the select few names the Directors allowed Marsh to retain. The name was lost in May 1923 when No. 52 was rebuilt to a 'B4x', but re-appeared briefly for the official photograph of 'B4x' No. 50 when it emerged from rebuilding in the works in June 1923, painted and lined out on the right-hand side only!**

Plate 5 : **Another corner of New Cross with locomotives alongside an early prefabricated structure, iron framed and clad in corrugated iron, once part of the carriage shed there. The photograph provides a contrast between a 'Terrier' and its younger brother, the 'D' Class tank. To the left is No. 56 *Shoreditch*, used on the East London line service, then 'D' No. 35 *Southwark*, which had come in from West Croydon where it had been based for most of the pre-Grouping period, and shortlived No. 8 *Brockley* (see page 143, top) of New Cross, which was withdrawn in April 1904 and broken up three months later.**

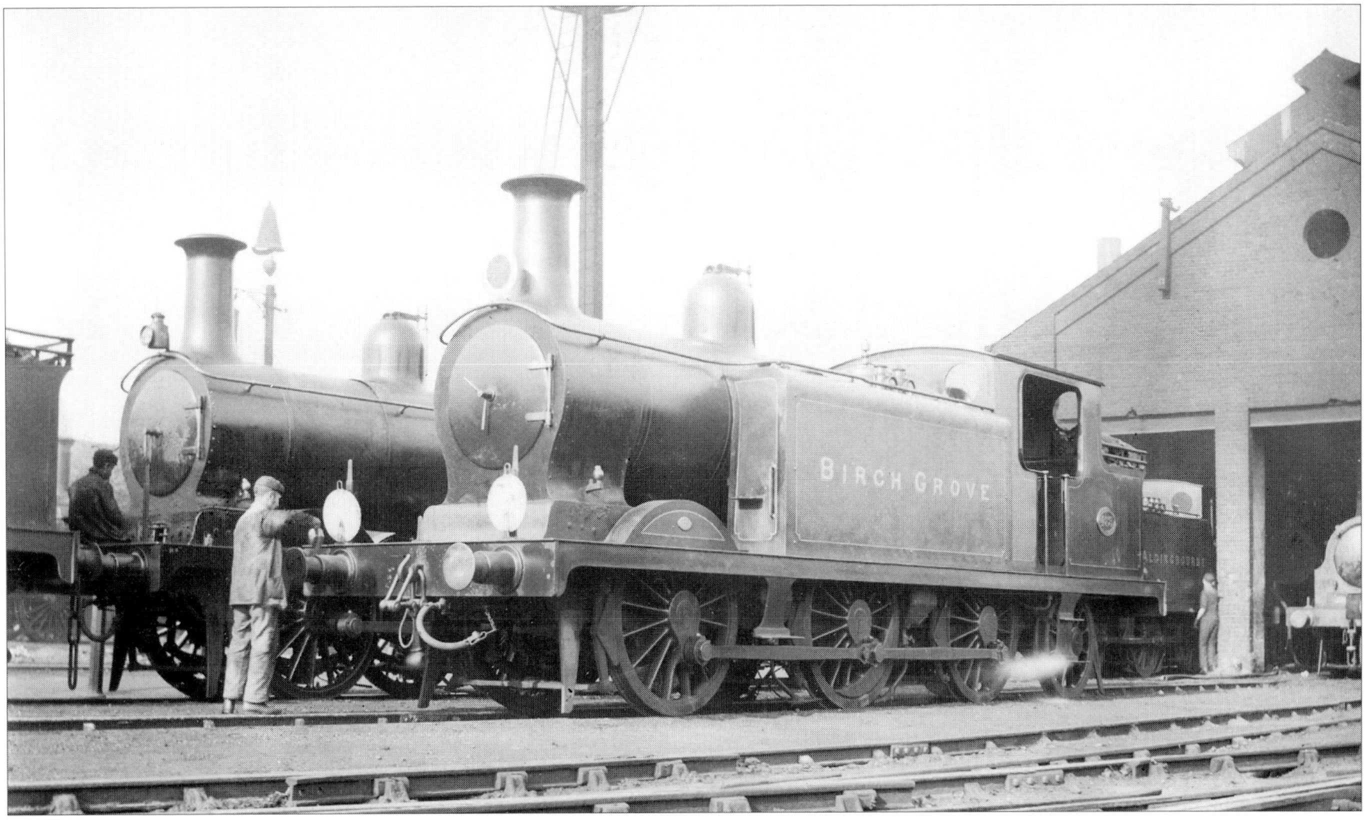

Plate 6 : **This now well-known photograph of 'E4' Class No. 473 *Birch Grove* was a Bennett picture, and the only Robert Billinton locomotive to survive on today's Bluebell Railway, most aptly since it was named after a hamlet and mansion near Horsted Keynes, latterly the home of late Prime Minister Harold Macmillan. Here it is seen in Stroudley's improved engine green, not goods green, as evidenced by the quite clear lining in the incised corner style.**

Plate 7 : **'Terrier' No. 62 *Martello* is taken from a less usual vantage point, enabling a glance round the corner of the shed foreman's office. In view is the north frontage of the Fitters Shop and behind it the smithy and site of the later carriage and wagon repair shop. The ancient vertical boilered crane was used to assist at the coaling stage. *Martello* still survives today, preserved at Bressingham and is often hired out on loan to run on other heritage lines.**

Plate 8 : **'D' Class tank No. 20 *Carshalton* in the carriage sidings at New Cross. It was renumbered 79 in February 1907. During this period the timekeeping of the class had proved erratic and in 1910, Marsh decided to experiment using a high pitched boiler, a circular smokebox and saddle, higher cab but reduced chimney and dome with coal rails added to the bunker.**

Plate 9 : **The super 'D' , now No. 79A and classed as 'D1x', is shown in its new form in one of the Bennett's later pictures again at New Cross. Though it might appear to be numbered A79, all sources refer to it as 79A. It was further renumbered to 349 in June 1913, 216 in December 1920 and, as the odd man out, succumbed to an early withdrawal in August 1933.**

Plate 10 : **Another Brighton survivor, 'Terrier' 0-6-0T No. 55 *Stepney*, taking coal by the stage at New Cross in 1903, soon after renumbering to 655. It was transferred to Brighton the following year after nearly thirty years of intensive service on the South London and East London suburban lines. Bennett's portrait provides a glimpse into another little photographed corner of the many faceted facilities of the New Cross sheds. The old Croydon shed is just visible on the right.**

Plate 11 : **Lawson Billinton had ordered seven boilers with top feed housed in the second dome to fit to his final batch of 'K' Class Moguls. The first reached Brighton Works on 14th March 1920 and, as the frames still had to be cut for the first of the new 'K's, it was allotted to No. 339, then in shops for a new firebox, and photographed by Walter at New Cross around the time of the Grouping. Walter continued his interest through to Nationalisation days, moving into LMS territory, joining the Stephenson Locomotive Society and participating extensively on shed visits.**

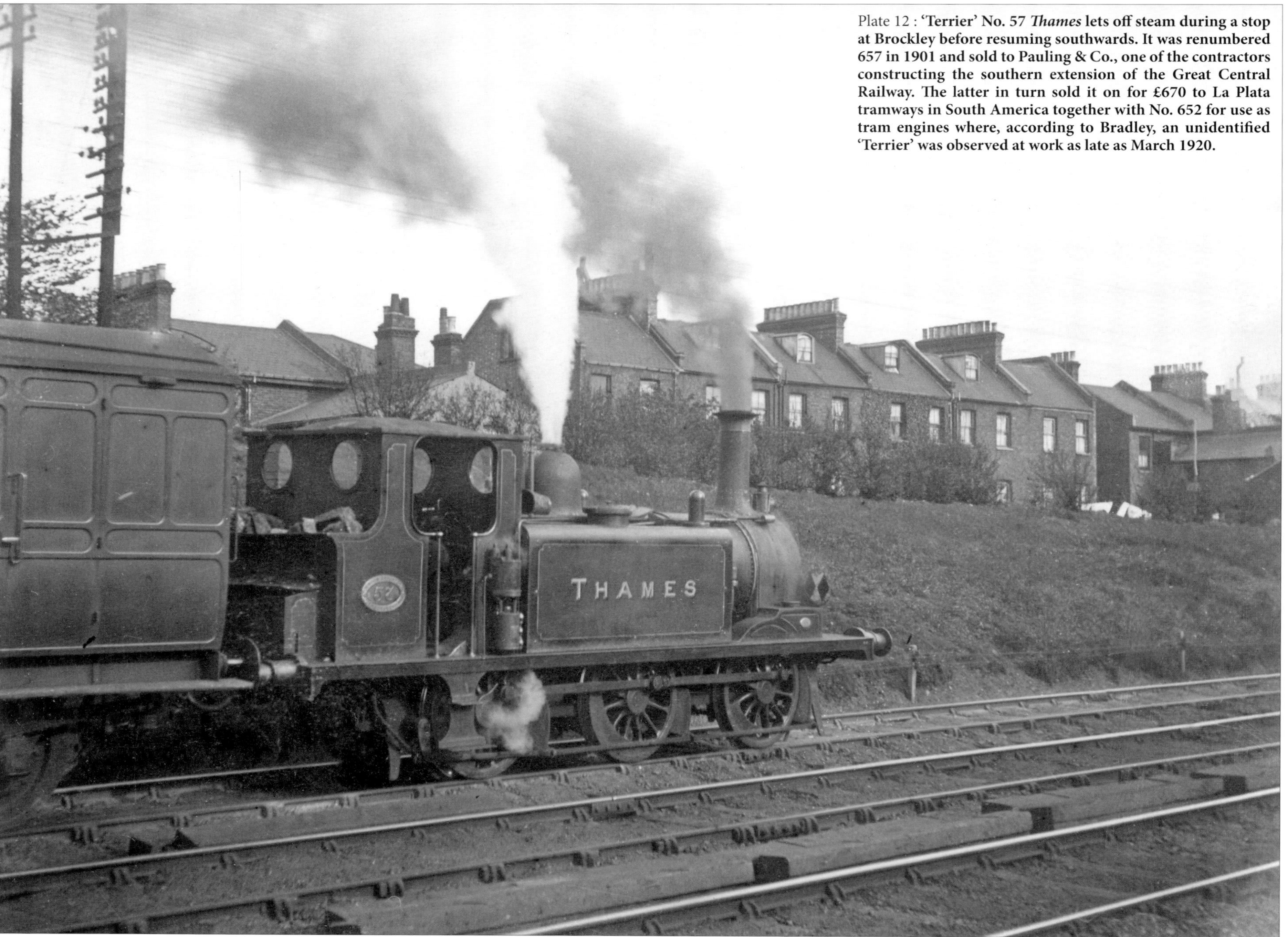

Plate 12 : 'Terrier' No. 57 *Thames* lets off steam during a stop at Brockley before resuming southwards. It was renumbered 657 in 1901 and sold to Pauling & Co., one of the contractors constructing the southern extension of the Great Central Railway. The latter in turn sold it on for £670 to La Plata tramways in South America together with No. 652 for use as tram engines where, according to Bradley, an unidentified 'Terrier' was observed at work as late as March 1920.

Plate 13 : **A Lyons 'D2' Class 0-4-2, a class rarely photographed on trains in motion, approaches Brockley Station with an Up train on the Up centre road. The station opened on 6th March 1871 in response to expanding commuter development, seen in the background, the two platforms only served the Up and Down slow lines.**

Plate 14 : **During the station stop at Brockley the fireman of 'D' Class tank No. 285 *Holmwood* replenishes the firebox with more coal. It stands at the Down slow platform, providing a glimpse of the neat LB&SC signal box which opened in 1886 and was closed in 1950. The signalman looks out at his signals which are in slotted posts with independent rotating lamps.**

Plate 15 : **Written on the reverse of the original is '*Goldsmid* going through East Croydon c1904'. This was 'B2' Class No. 316 of Fratton shed. The signal gantry behind the train is controlled from the North box, provided in 1896, situated just beyond the platform end. On the immediate right is an excellent view of Victoria Wharf, Hall & Co's extensive yard, the backcloth to many photographs taken from the north end of the platforms. The name New Croydon was dropped in 1909, the eastern part of the station being known as East Croydon Local.**

Plate 16 : **Yet another 'D' Class, No. 276 *Rudgwick* of Battersea Shed stands with others in the spare middle siding at East Croydon Station. On the platform above the locomotive's buffers is one of the then commonplace high backed benches of which the LB&SCR was extremely fond, since it provided some good protection against the elements. There were examples at East Grinstead (High Level) until demolition, and the author saw the very last of these a few years back at Battersea Park Station.**

Plate 17 : **This well known portrait of 'E4' Class No. 488 has on the reverse 'SERIES PUBLISHED BY W. BENNETT, HOVE'. *Oakwood*, based at West Croydon, whose allocation consisted of suburban passenger tank engines and pick-up goods locomotives, stands at the shunting neck to the locomotive yard and shed there. No. 488's crew as listed in 1905 were Driver Frederick Ladd and Fireman Alfred Spooner. It lost its name in 1910, being returned to its initial allocation at New Cross Shed.** ***courtesy Lawrence Marshall collection***

Plate 18 : **Marsh H1 class Atlantic No. 38 awaits its next duty in the middle road at East Croydon. To get some urgently needed more powerful express engines on the road, Marsh sent for a set of Great Northern Railway drawings from Doncaster, where he had previously worked as second-in-command to H. A. Ivatt. No. 38, built by Kitson & Co. of Leeds, was delivered to enter traffic in December 1905 and assigned to Brighton shed in the care of Driver William Vallance. It catches the interest of spectators on both platforms. No. 38 lasted to the class's end in July 1951 with over a million miles to its credit.**

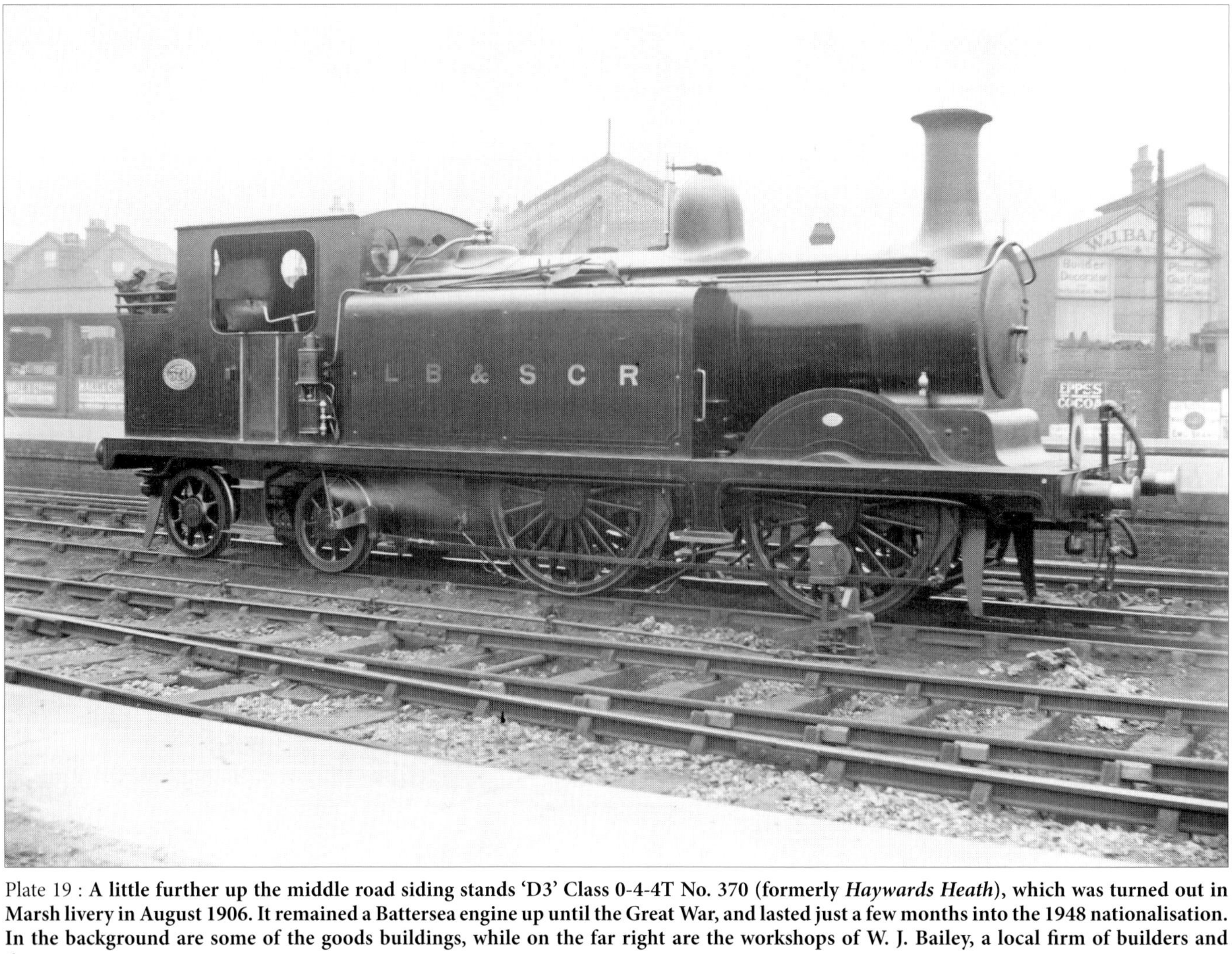

Plate 19 : **A little further up the middle road siding stands 'D3' Class 0-4-4T No. 370 (formerly *Haywards Heath*), which was turned out in Marsh livery in August 1906. It remained a Battersea engine up until the Great War, and lasted just a few months into the 1948 nationalisation. In the background are some of the goods buildings, while on the far right are the workshops of W. J. Bailey, a local firm of builders and decorators.**

Plate 20 : **'E4' Class radial tank No. 490 *Bohemia*, named after a district in Hastings, seems very much at home and bearing the shortlived 'STON' before the renaming of the station to Coulsdon North & Smitham Downs on 1st June 1911 with the shed code becoming 'COULS'. The latter dated from 1899 when the line was quadrupled from South Croydon. No. 490 was allocated there from mid-1904 to 1910 when, without its name, it was returned to its previous posting at New Cross Shed.**

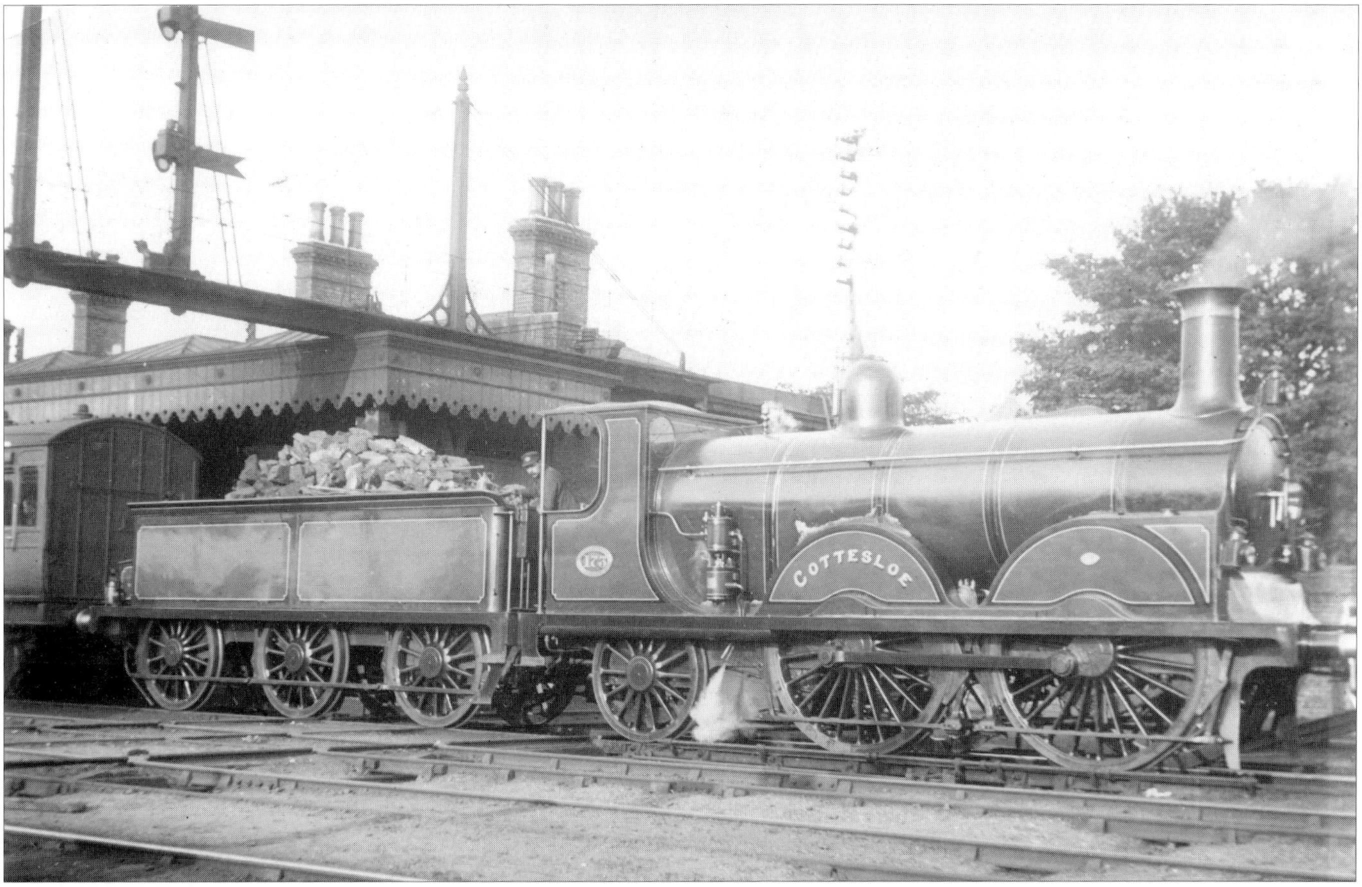

Plate 21 : **The South Eastern & Chatham Railway was the dominant company at Redhill, the focal point of its lines to Tonbridge and Reading, the result of the Government forcing the London & Brighton Railway to sell the Stoats Nest-Redhill (then Reigate Junction) section to the South Eastern Railway, though the former's traffic greatly exceeded that of the latter. Inevitably friction ensued, gaining it the nickname 'Stopham Junction'. Finally at the turn of the century the LB&SCR decided to bypass Redhill by constructing its Quarry line. 'Gladstone' No. 173 *Cottesloe* of New Cross Shed stands at the Down platform with a semi-fast to Brighton. Note too, the fine oversailing SER bracket signal.**

Plate 22 : **Several photographs of 'Terrier' No. 83 *Earlswood* were taken of it standing in Redhill South Yard with the town's gas holder in the background. 'Terrier' historians from Bradley downwards make much of the fact that this locomotive carried the code EARLS on its frames, but in none of the photographs portrayed here or elsewhere does this appear so. Renumbered 683 in 1912, it was sold in 1918 to the War Office for Admiralty use at Inverness. They in turn sold it to the Shropshire & Montgomery Railway in November 1923 for £470, becoming its No. 9 *Daphne*. The wheel came round full circle when in January 1939 it found its way back to Eastleigh where it spent WW2, possibly supplying spare parts to the surviving 'Terriers'. Scrapping eventually took place in April 1949.**

courtesy Lawrence Marshall collection

Plate 23 : **This is from an original quarter plate and shows Marsh Atlantic No. 38 racing through the newly rebuilt station at Earlswood with an Up express which includes three Pullmans. No. 38 was a Brighton engine, given into Driver William Vallance's care when first entering traffic in December 1905. The terrace of cottages in the background is still in existence.**

Plate 24 : **Looking south at Earlswood this view is taken from the Up local platform which extends far beyond the other platforms here. The train of mainly goods empties stands in the Middle Siding in between the fast and slow lines with Billinton 'C2' Class 0-6-0 No. 446 of New Cross in Marsh colours at its head. Earlswood Station box, opened in 1906 and closed in 1932 with the Brighton electrification and consequent resignalling, is visible on the right.**

Plate 25 : ***Earlswood*** **was based at its namesake, only journeying down to Three Bridges for boiler washouts and minor repairs. Here it stands by the entrance gate to the Asylum siding with a porter/signalman in attendance to operate it. It was used to bring in coal for Earlswood Asylum for Idiots, later renamed the Royal Earlswood Institution. It has been pointed out that the Down main starting signal is shown lowered. The siding had no shunting spur outside of the gate but ran directly into the Down main. Access from Redhill South Yard to the Asylum siding must have blocked the main line for several minutes.**

Plate 26 : **A quartet of locomotives stand on the spur line linking, by means of a reversal, the low level second locomotive shed at Three Bridges to the main line. They are from the left 'E4' Class No. 465 *Hurst Green* and 'E1' Class tanks No. 143 *Nuremberg*, and No. 109 *Strasbourg*, and 'E3' No. 170 *Bishopstone*. The building to the rear is the roof and retaining wall of the western island platform of the pre-widening Three Bridges Station. A very young Bennett son is seen posed in front of *Strasbourg*.**

Plate 27 : **A pleasantly posed scene featuring shed staff outside the Three Bridges second shed which was at a lower level than the main line. D tank No. 258 *Cosham* was a regular there for forty years, apart from a brief posting to Horsham. Note the station roof on the up side behind the second engine. *Cosham* was an early conversion, still carrying its name and the Marsh buffer beam number, confirmed by the writing on the reverse of the print; circa 1906.**

Plate 28 : **The last Craven engine to survive on the LB&SCR, thanks to an assignment to Three Bridges for pumping duty. It arrived carrying its second number 466 on 23rd April 1897, was renumbered 514 the following March to make way for the 'E4' series, only to be changed again to 614 in May 1899. At this stage the dome cover has been lifted off and placed between dome and chimney so that a feed water pipe could be inserted into the side of the inner dome in similar practice to Lawson Billinton's top feed system. A tall vent has been placed just behind the cab spectacle plate.**

Plate 29 : **'Terrier' No. 38 *Millwall* taken in 1904. The following June it was renumbered 638. It took up the pumping duty at Three Bridges on 6th July 1901, replacing the Craven engine seen above. Following completion of a separate pump house, the 'Terrier' was towed away on 11th October 1905 to Brighton, but evaded scrap, becoming works pilot through to 1918 (see page 10). That February it was sold for £1,200 for Admiralty use at Invergordon, was noted in store at the Government Surplus Material Depot at Dalmuir in Scotland, and two years later was sold to the Shropshire & Montgomery Railway for £470 as its No. 8 *Dido* until laid aside in 1930 before being sold for scrap in October 1934.** ***courtesy Lawrence Marshall collection***

Plate 30 : 'Gladstone' No. 218 *Beaconsfield*, named after Benjamin Disraeli following his peerage, stands at the end of the down platform under the imposing triple-posted signal gantry that straddled the south end of Three Bridges Station. This was the only lattice post signal of this type on the LB&SCR. No. 218 was a Brighton engine throughout. The photograph must have been taken prior to December 1906 when it lost its name. It was an early casualty of the class, being withdrawn in June 1913. The first vehicle in the train is a Billinton double ended brake van.

Plate 31 : **'B1' Class 0-4-2 No. 179 (*Sandown* until December 1905) enters the cutting leading to the north portal of Balcombe Tunnel with an excursion special of eighteen carriages and carrying a Brighton 'special' headcode on its way to the seaside, albeit in the winter or early spring. A clearly discerned path climbing up on the right may have been of assistance to the Bennetts in reaching this point.**

Plate 32 : **Same location, different date and with the time around midday, judging from the lighting, new 'I1' Class 4-4-2T No. 597 of Brighton shed, which entered traffic in December 1906, heads for Balcombe Tunnel and back to base in charge of a semi-fast service. R. E. L. Maunsell rebuilt the under-performing class between 1925 and 1932 to give them a new lease of life, and they were able to soldier on into the war years. No. 597 lasted until 1946.**

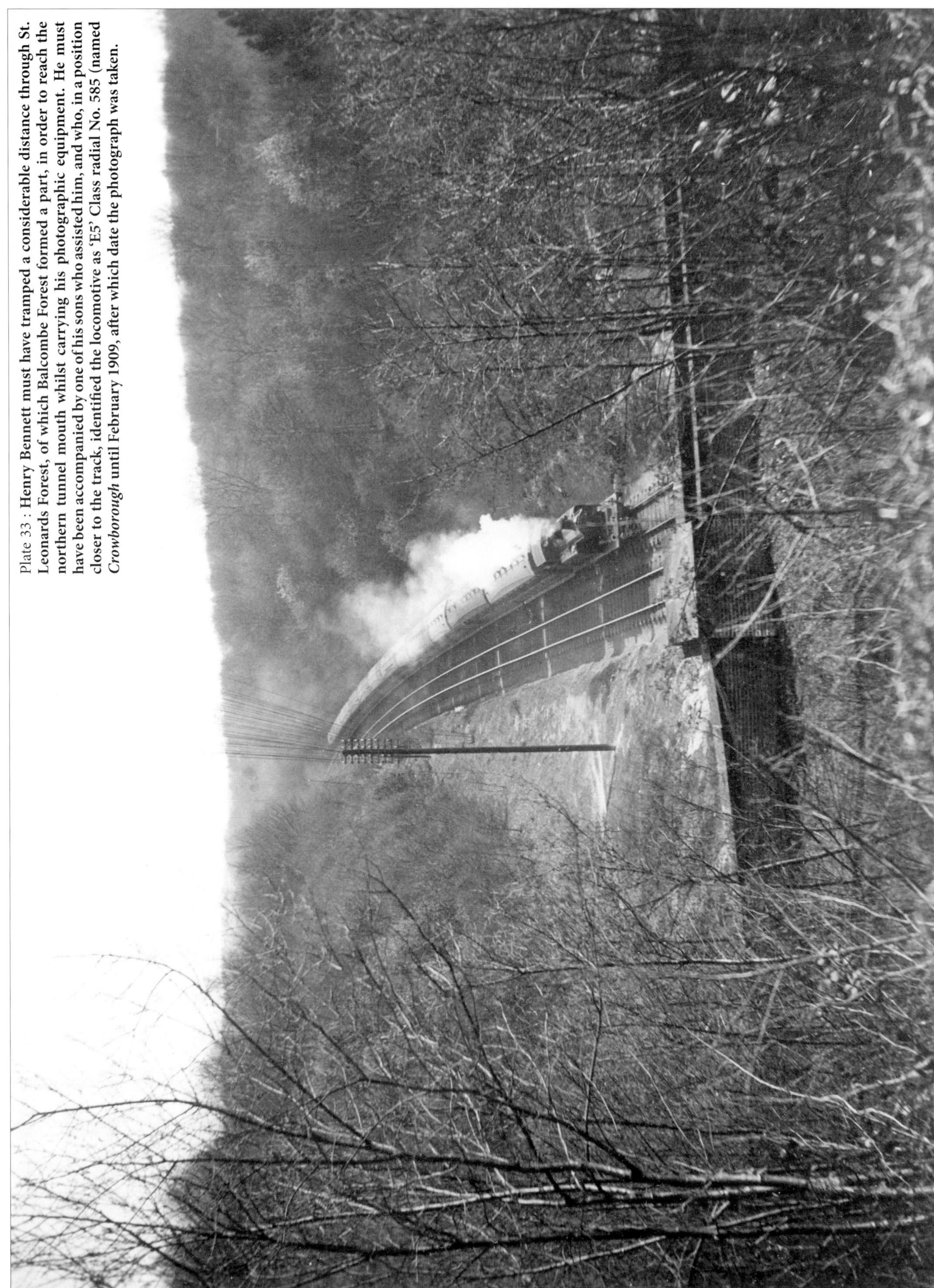

Plate 33 : **Henry Bennett must have tramped a considerable distance through St. Leonards Forest, of which Balcombe Forest formed a part, in order to reach the northern tunnel mouth whilst carrying his photographic equipment. He must have been accompanied by one of his sons who assisted him, and who, in a position closer to the track, identified the locomotive as 'E5' Class radial No. 585 (named *Crowborough* until February 1909, after which date the photograph was taken.**

Plate 34 : **With Balcombe Forest on the skyline behind the tall LB&SCR signal, 'B2' Class No. 209 *Wolfe Barry* heads a coast bound express past Copyhold Junction. John Wolfe Barry was the engineer who surveyed and supervised the construction of the Lewes & East Grinstead Railway, a branch of which ran from Horsted Keynes through Ardingly to join the Brighton main line at this point.**

Plate 35 : **During his time at Copyhold Bridge, Bennett was able to photograph a train coming off the Ardingly line. Looking north, 'Gladstone' 0-4-2 No. 193 (formerly *Fremantle*), running tender first, brings a local from the East Grinstead line bound for Haywards Heath. No. 193 was a Battersea based locomotive, reboilered in 1906 with Ramsbottom safety valves, re-emerging from overhaul on 17th February 1907.**

Plate 36 : **The line to Ardingly curves away from Copyhold Junction through the fields of Rivers Farm, while the line of trees in the middle distance marks the course of the ill-fated Ouse Valley railway of 1864-7. 'B4' Class No. 58 *Kitchener* speeds a southbound express which includes the proverbial Pullman car.**

Plate 37 : **The oddly numbered 'B2' Class No. 171, named *Nevill* until August 1907, and a Brighton engine until moved to St. Leonards in 1904, shuts off steam for the stop at Haywards Heath, the north sidings of which are seen in the foreground. The setting is the four track section through Copyhold cutting which extended from Copyhold Junction seen in the previous photographs. Note the tall gantry signal up on the bank (right). The carriages are carrying the Marsh umber and white livery introduced in 1905.**

Plate 38 : **Taken from the bridge seen in the previous photograph and in the opposite direction, a 'B2' Class 4-4-0 is leaving Haywards Heath, seen in the distance. The headcode appears to be that of a train for Kensington via the Quarry Line, originating from Brighton. All of the carriage are LB&SC Billinton stock apart from the lower roofed vehicle which is by Stroudley. A number carry the Marsh umber and white livery.**

Plate 39 : **The Sunny South Special, a through train off the London & North Western Railway which was inaugurated in this form in 1905. The train is comprised of 50ft arc roofed stock and a 65ft 6in. clerestory roof dining car. The train is made up of two portions, the forward part with the restaurant car from Manchester and the rear from Liverpool and served Brighton and Eastbourne. The locomotive is a gleaming 'B4' Class, No. 54, often used for Royal specials. The former *Empress* was renamed *Princess Royal* in August 1906, departing from Brighton shops in Marsh livery in October that same year. Haywards Heath emerged as a new dormitory town, thanks to the arrival of the railway, and the new development, close to the station, can be seen on the right.**

Plate 40 : **'E5' Class No. 575 *Westergate*, running as a 2-4-2T, enters Haywards Heath from the north with a service to Brighton, its home base, comprised of a seven coach Billinton suburban block set. The photograph is taken before 1910. Of particular interest in this picture is the pit for the turntable (far left) of the original short-lived shed. The turntable was moved to the Down side from this original shed located on the Up side. There was a water tower and coaling facilities, the actual shed being closed and converted to a goods shed in 1876, still retaining its louvres in the roof.**

Plate 41 : **The same locomotive, again at Haywards Heath, this time on humbler duties shunting the south yard on the down side with a partial glimpse of a private owner wagon from Groombridge. The backcloth suggests that sawn timber and planking was a major player in goods brought on to the railway. The shunter standing by has an excellent view of the 2-4-2 wheel arrangement which pertained from 1909. J. N. Maskelyne gives 1909 as the date of the shortlived conversion but, after numerous complaints, those members of the class so transformed were all back to 0-6-2T by September that year.**

Plate 42 : **Photographs taken at the south end of 240 yard Haywards Heath Tunnel are few and far between, and understandably so, for making this location presented some difficulty. Here the down Southern Belle emerges from the south portal c1909, hauled by Marsh Atlantic No. 41. It was one of the wartime casualties of the class, being withdrawn in March 1944.**

Plate 43 : **No. 41 again, a couple of miles further south, where the Brighton main line runs straight as a die for much of its length, hurrying the down Pullman Limited beneath the high Ashenground bridge, south of Haywards Heath. The thickly wooded land bordering the track is the remains of the old forest that covered much of the High Weald in contrast to the bare downland further south. The 50 mile run to Brighton was scheduled for an hour or, to be exact, 59 minutes for trains left Victoria a minute after the advertised starting time to give their patrons that vital extra minute!**

Plate 44 : **Stroudley 'G' Class single No. 331 *Fairlight* approaches Keymer Junction cautiously from the north (note the distant junction signal is still on), as it prepares for the sharp curve with its lengthy excursion train from London Bridge to Hastings in early Edwardian days. The approach to the junction lies in a shallow cutting with Wivelsfield Station and signal box behind the rear of the train, and serving the adjacent hamlet named World's End.**

Plate 45 : **A partial glimpse of Keymer or Wivelsfield Junction signal box, mounted on stilts. The box was opened in 1862-3 and was replaced in 1913. The exceptional height enabled the signalman to see over the road bridge to the left of the junction. It remained in use until about 1912. The little white post protruding out of the bank just beyond the steps carried the name and marked the division of lengths between adjacent teams of gangers. In this against the light shot 'C3' Class 0-6-0 No. 307 traverses the junction with an Up goods of empties. Its allocated driver when new in August 1906 was Harry Mitchell of Brighton shed.**

Plate 46 : **Rounding the sharp curve towards Lewes at Keymer Junction with an excursion to Hastings is 'E5' Class No. 406 *Colworth*. Entering traffic on 23rd November 1904 and based at Brighton in the charge of Driver Frank Smith, No. 406 passes the site of the original Keymer Junction Station situated on the Lewes line curve immediately after the junction.**

Plate 47 : **Class 'B4' No. 60 (*Kimberley* until October 1905) heads the heavy 8.10am from Brighton, unofficially known as the Breadwinners train. It is seen entering Burgess Hill from the south past the graceful and lofty signal box built in 1875 astride the goods shed road which had a deviation to pass under the box to the yard on the Up side. With its elegant staircase it stands 100 yards from the end of the Up platform. A 1930s photograph shows the track which ran under the box still having the deviation, even though the box itself had been replaced in 1926.**

Plate 48 : **A self-conscious porter eyes the camera, with the proverbial milk churns farther up the platform, as 'B4' Class No. 69 (formerly *Bagshot*) passes through Burgess Hill Station at high speed. The single storey main buildings on the overbridge at the London end of the station date from alterations made in 1877 to replace the previous station buildings, a number of which were still in existence until the 1980s as coal offices and parcel stores. The earliest date for this photograph is 1907.**

Plate 49 : **Although undated this poor but rare snow scene, taken in the shallow cutting south of Hassocks Station, is inscribed on reverse: 'The "old" *Cornwall*', and is of great interest as it is only the second known view of a 'Richmond' class locomotive in action and is previously unpublished. It dates to after 1899-1900 as the leading vehicle is a Billinton bogie full brake to diagram 226. Locomotive No. 210 of the 'Richmond' class, so named after the first member, entered service in September 1879. It was involved in an accident at Stoats Nest on 10th December 1890 when a wagon had been left out on the main line during shunting operations. Renumbered 510 in 1897 and 610 in 1900, it yielded its name so that the new 'B4' Class 4-4-0 No. 74 could carry that illustrious title, and received in return an equally distinguished name *Belgravia*.**

Plate 50 : **John Minnis has described the north portal of Clayton Tunnel as one of the most delightful follies in England. Many theories have been advanced as to the reasons for the design of the castellated portal, ranging from its possible use in an invasion to its re-assuring the passenger for the long dark journey ahead. Certainly the addition of a cottage on the top c1850 was a stroke of genius by a man who had an eye, perhaps unconsciously, for the picturesque. The express emerging from the 2259 yard long tunnel is headed by 'B4' Class No. 44 *Cecil Rhodes* in this c1906 photograph.**

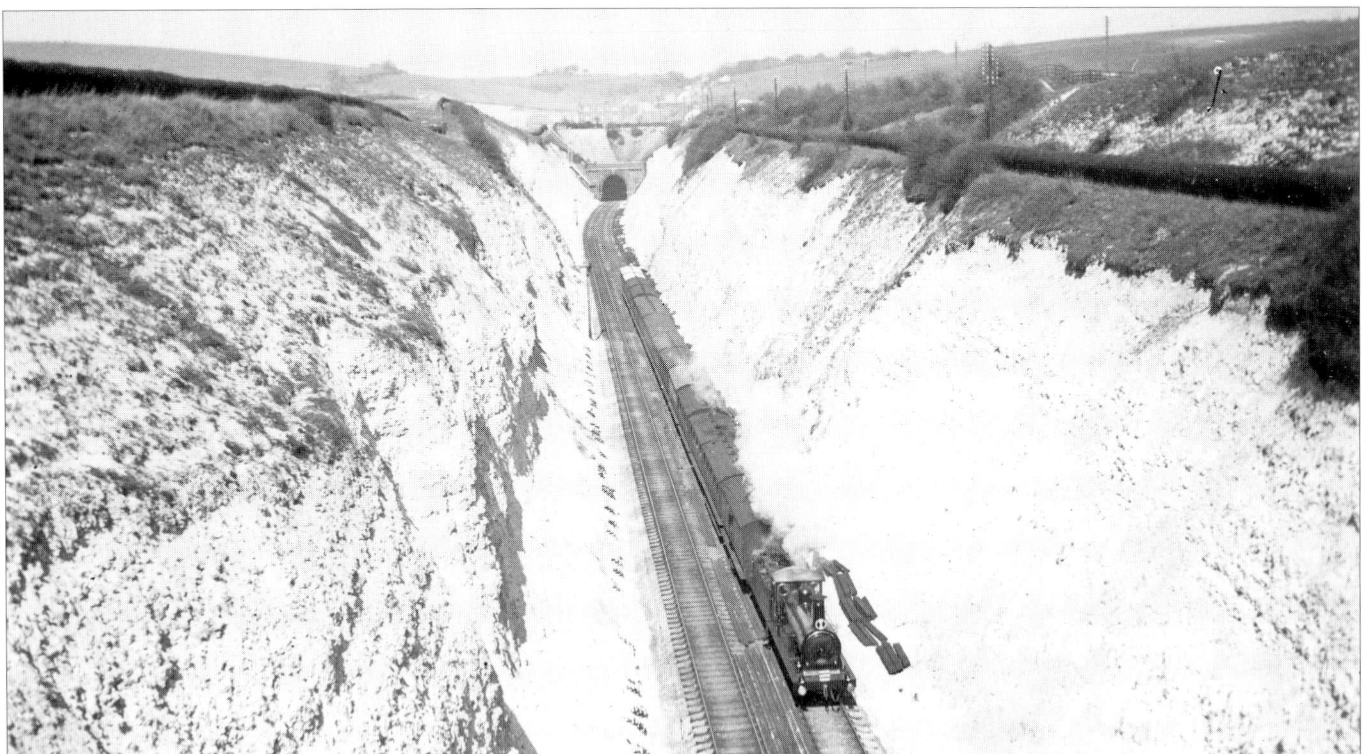

Plate 51 : **The turn of the century was the heyday of seaside excursions, and each summer weekend a procession of specials would steam down the main line to the various coastal resorts. 'G' Class 2-2-2 No. 333 *Ventnor* heads a Littlehampton bound excursion special, having cleared Clayton Tunnel, the south entrance of which can be clearly seen with its small signal cabin to the left and its accompanying flight of stairs accessing the main road. The track is in course of being relaid, as indicated by the array of rail lengths between the tracks and the sleepers deposited near the bottom of the side of the imposing chalk cutting.**

Plate 52 : **This attractive picture was taken from a farm occupation bridge near Scare Hill, carrying a lane from the main parallel London-Brighton Road, a mere stone's throw away behind the ridge on the right. The locomotive is 'B4' Class No. 54 *Princess Royal*, formerly the proud *Empress* until it entered works in 1906 for transformation to Marsh umber, receiving its new name in August and re-entering service on 17th October the same year. The second vehicle is a Stroudley radial First, one of twelve delivered in 1880 and photographically very elusive.**

Plate 53 : **Scare Hill Bridge again as 'H1' Class No. 38 speeds through the chalk cuttings of the South Downs near Patcham with a train composed, apart from the Pullman car, of Marsh's elliptical roof stock in the beautiful but short lived umber and white livery c1909. While grass has covered most of the original chalk banks, there are indications of some recent chalk erosion.**

Plate 54 : **This study of 'Gladstone' No. 199 *Samuel Laing*, (named after one of the company's most notable and long serving chairmen) bursting out of the north end of Patcham Tunnel with a pair of Marsh elliptical coaches immediately behind the engine, includes a glimpse of a pair of railway cottages (right) which remain virtually unaltered today. The distant signal displays the LB&SC practice of painting the arm red with a white stripe.**

Plate 55 : **The Down Pullman Limited approaching Preston Park hauled by a 'B4' Class 4-4-0. Note the widening work and ballast wagons, used for the removal of chalk, with a brake van at each end, and also the fine tall gantry of signals just north of the station.**

Plate 56 : **'D' Class tank No. 290 *Denbies* was transferred from Dorking to Brighton shed in October 1897. Here in umber livery, received in May 1907, it is in charge of the 6.50am to Haywards Heath, formed of a main line Marsh elliptical set as it passes the Preston chalk banks with work in full progress on widening to allow additional carriage sidings to be laid. In Ralph Stent's words: '*Very interesting, for it clearly shows trucks with dumb buffers (but they did make a noise!). They had canvas covers to keep the ballast out of the axle boxes*'. They were still in use during the Great War and up to the Grouping although such buffers had been banned for main line work beyond 1914.**

Plate 57 : **A 'D' Class tank in idyllic surroundings photographed at Preston Park. No. 297 *Bonchurch* was used as Paint shop pilot and may be resting from its duties. This portrait is taken a decade after the catastrophic Mayfield accident (See page 141), but prior to December 1908 when it went through works and in its new Marsh livery was posted to Horsham shed. Note the tightly railed fencing and the newly painted linesman's hut.**

Plate 58 : **'Gladstone' No. 198 *Sheffield* (named after the Bluebell railway's Lord Sheffield) passes buildings that were to become the Pullman car works at Preston Park with a train of Billinton stock c1903, including one vehicle in the experimental green and white livery. The lines on the right are those of the Cliftonville spur built in 1879 to enable Worthing and west coast trains to avoid Brighton. The end coach in the siding next to the main line train curiously bears a discarded West Croydon name board upside down on its roof.**

Plate 59 : **A beautiful quality portrait of 'B4' Class 4-4-0 No. 49 *Queensland*, and a true 'Scotchman' at that, standing immaculate in all its glory. The pose and position of the headlamps suggest some kind of an official photograph, once again suggesting that Henry Bennett had inside information. The leafy location could well be on the east side of the running lines opposite Lovers Walk, and may well have been taken when the locomotive entered service in August 1901.**

Plate 60 : **A pleasant portrait of 'Terrier' No. 80 *Bookham* taken in Brighton Upper Goods yard. It was renumbered 680 in 1908 and equipped with Marsh motor train gear and rebuilt as an 'A1x' in April 1912. It was used with No. 643 in the Angus brake trials in 1920 and scrapped six years later.** ***courtesy Lawrence Marshall collection***

Plate 61 : **Sadly Robert Billinton had passed away the previous November but Henry Bennett was quick off the mark to get a picture of his latest posthumous creation. The first 'E6' Class No. 407 *Worplesdon* emerged from Brighton Works on 11th January 1905, allocated to New Cross as coded at the front of the buffer beam, and under the charge of Driver Thomas Woolnough. Marsh rebuilt No. 407 to Class 'E6x' in June 1911. The van in the background has louvres indicating it to be for Grande Vitesse traffic.**

Plate 62 : **The signals seen here were provided in 1881-2 as part of the major rebuilding of Brighton Station. 'E1' Class 0-6-0T No. 160 *Portslade*, a Brighton locomotive in home surroundings, shunting a lime-coated cattle wagon, several of which were habitually stabled in a siding alongside the coaling line next to Brighton shed. This portrait also affords a splendid view of the frontage of Brighton works and may date to c.1900.**

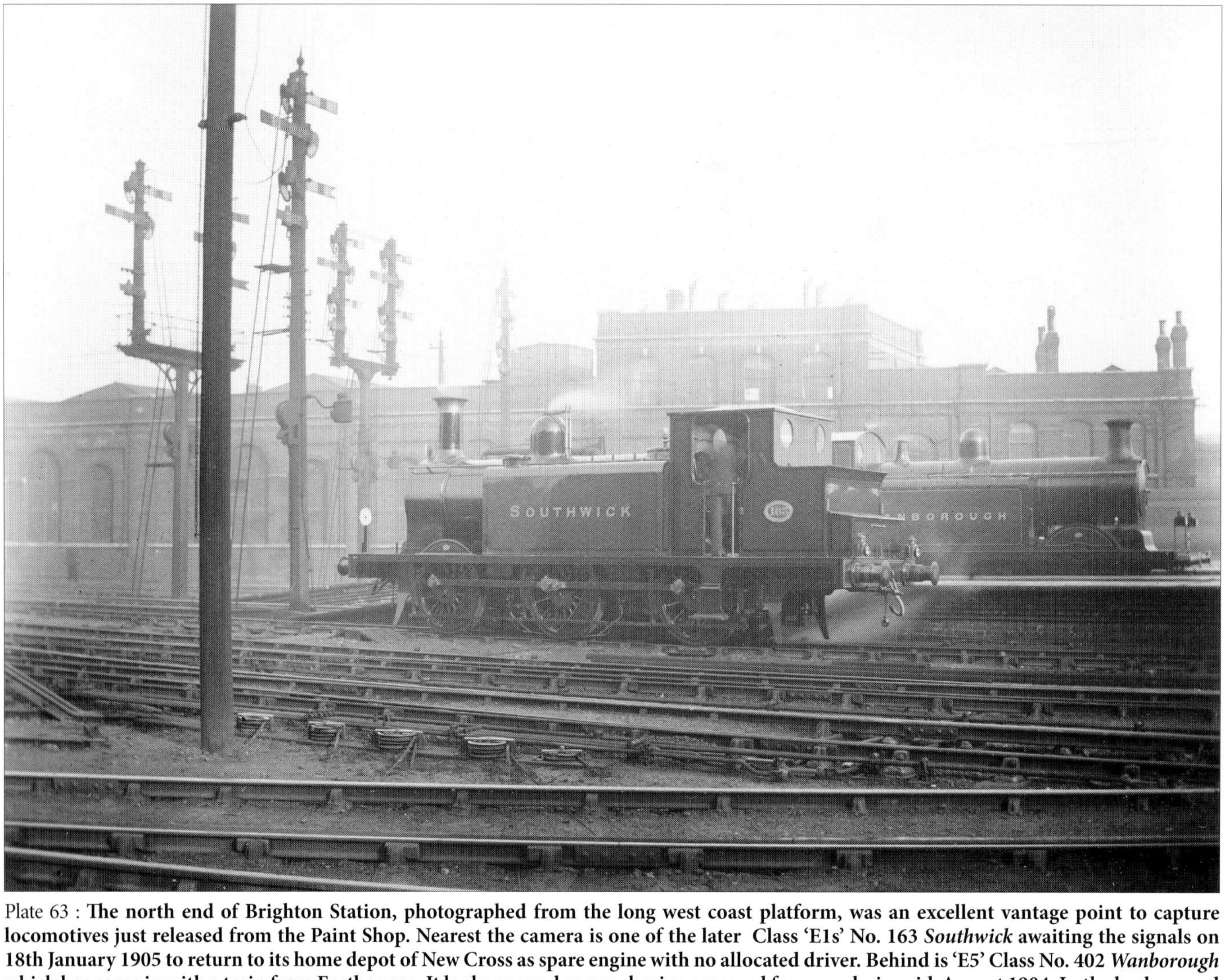

Plate 63 : **The north end of Brighton Station, photographed from the long west coast platform, was an excellent vantage point to capture locomotives just released from the Paint Shop. Nearest the camera is one of the later Class 'E1s' No. 163 *Southwick* awaiting the signals on 18th January 1905 to return to its home depot of New Cross as spare engine with no allocated driver. Behind is 'E5' Class No. 402 *Wanborough* which has come in with a train from Eastbourne. It looks as good as new, having emerged from works in mid-August 1904. In the background stands the frontage of Brighton works and at the platform ends a splendid array of bi-directional signals.**

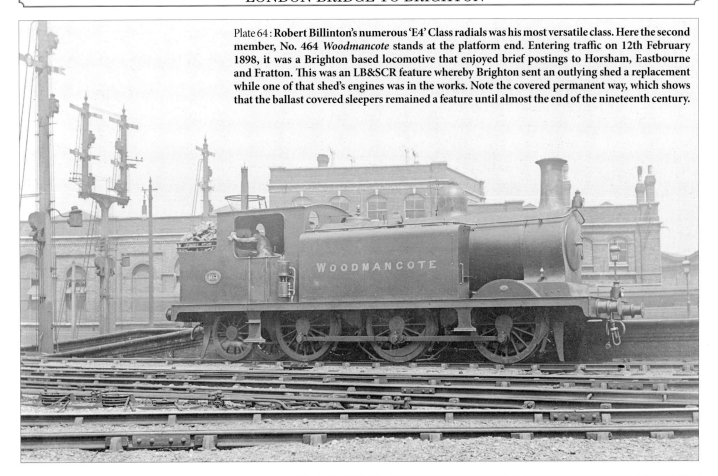

Plate 64 : **Robert Billinton's numerous 'E4' Class radials was his most versatile class. Here the second member, No. 464 *Woodmancote* stands at the platform end. Entering traffic on 12th February 1898, it was a Brighton based locomotive that enjoyed brief postings to Horsham, Eastbourne and Fratton. This was an LB&SCR feature whereby Brighton sent an outlying shed a replacement while one of that shed's engines was in the works. Note the covered permanent way, which shows that the ballast covered sleepers remained a feature until almost the end of the nineteenth century.**

Plate 65 : **A portrait of resplendent 'D' Class tank No. 225 *Ashbourne* receiving last minute attention under the station roof at Brighton. Ralph Stent, who was also there to take this picture, has pencilled in on the reverse: '*Going out on trial trip with Charlie Peters, the test driver*'. It entered traffic in June 1885 and was based at Battersea Shed throughout the period up to World War One. It emerged from a works overhaul, which ties in with its pristine condition, on 1st February 1905, fortunate to retain its name before Marsh sorted out his livery policy later in the year.**

Plate 66 : **The Nursery at Brighton on a Bank Holiday in 1904. The former driver William Coney writes: '*I have stood on this platform when the above young man was a porter. These engines have all brought excursionists to Brighton. The trains were so frequent that there was no room for all the engines to turn on shed and then return. So they would all couple up and proceed to Preston Park, then down the Cliftonville curve to Hove and back as seen here, all turned round*'. The line is led by 'D2' Class 0-4-2 *Splugen* and contains three other class members. The odd man out is 'D3, Class 0-4-4T No. 371 *Angmering*.**

Plate 67 : **'G' Class Single No. 346 *Alfriston* stands at the end of Brighton Station's Platform No. 9, released after its coaching stock has been taken to London Road sidings. It has brought down a special (double diamond headcode discs) via the Quarry line (square board with horizontal bands), which opened on 1st April 1900 to passenger services. As to the gentleman on view, could this be Henry Bennett photographed by one of his sons? Whatever, the photograph provides a close view of the grand frontage of Brighton works with the windows above the engine's boiler housing the administrative offices giving a grandstand view of the station approaches and across towards the neck of the engine shed.**

Courtesy Lawrence Marshall collection

Plate 68 : **Marsh 'H1' Atlantic rests close to the buffer stops under the magnificent glass roof of Brighton terminus with a run from London via the Quarry line as shown by the distinctive square headcode. Entering traffic in February 1906, and still a novelty, small wonder that two young station porters should choose to pose down on the track beside the engine, which has also caught the admiration of people on the platform.**

SUTTON'S SEEDS
Remington
TYPEWRITER
BASS
BASS
SUTTON'S SEEDS
EPPS'S
WATERLOO
CAKES

Opposite: Plate 69 : **Another end of the road picture as 'D' Class tank No. 21 *Beddington* stands at rest at the easternmost platform at Brighton, having brought in a passenger working from its home town of Tunbridge Wells. The picture is taken after the last shopping in May 1905 and prior to the one in 1909 when it lost its name. The Edwardian passenger must have been overwhelmed by the array of advertisements. Suttons Seeds must have paid the railway well. Other enamel plaques are for ales, cakes, cocoa, inks, typewriters and furniture storage.**

Plate 70 : **The brand new pioneer Marsh 'C3' Class goods 0-6-0 No. 300 is transferred from the paint shop to the running shed at Brighton by 'E1' Class tank No. 159 *Edenbridge*. The sheen of the Marsh lined black goods livery contrasts with the dull black used on the smoke box which has yet to receive its final coat. No. 300 entered traffic in March 1906, and at this point was probably being prepared for a trial trip.**

Plate 71 : **Henry Bennett was there to record the visits to Brighton in 1909 of the L&NWR's unsuperheated 'Precursor' Class 4-4-0 No. 7 *Titan* which fared so unfavourably in comparison to the Marsh 'I3' Class Atlantic tanks. The latter won hands down in the key areas of coal and water consumption. Derek Cross saw the triumph in an even wider context: '*The Brighton gave the lordly L&NWR a bloody nose, but proved the merits of superheating to contemporary locomotive engineers*'.**

Plate 72 : **A panoramic view of Brighton Shed on a Sunday morning was a dream picture for any railway photographer, and Henry Bennett was no exception. Taken over the wall atop the chalk cliff overhanging the shed from Howard Place that runs steeply up from Brighton Station and then just as sharply down to Montpelier Road and the shed entrance, the reader is left to feast on the scene and identify the various classes of locomotive.**

Plate 73 : **Shed photography was never easy in the cramped and crowded shadowy precincts but here we have a Bennett masterpiece. 'E4' Class 0-6-2T No. 565 *Littleton* commenced working from Battersea Shed as an oil burner on 1st May 1902, using the Bell & Holden injector system. The oil tank can be seen on the bunker. Following trials in the London area, it was allocated to Horsham Shed. Artistically posed in a setting between columns and which includes a decorative lamp and bracket, its superb state of turnout betokens the fact that it was still a comparatively new engine, being built in 1902. This fine portrait must have been taken before August 1903 when it was reconverted to coal burning.**

Plate 74 : **'A' Class No. 644 *Fulham* was the spare 'Terrier' covering half a dozen members of the class still based at Brighton Shed in the new century. Here it is seen responsible for shunting the wagons of engine coal at the depot, a function that the class continued to share over the next sixty years with the similarly diminutive ex SE&CR 'P' Class tanks. First allocated to Battersea, then after a brief spell at Midhurst, it was transferred to Brighton and on to the duplicate list in June 1900 and renumbered 644, remaining at Brighton until the Grouping.**

Plate 75 : **Henry Bennett, probably with inside information, was at hand to capture a historic moment and a unique picture of Kent & East Sussex Railway No. 5 *Rolvenden*, formerly No. 71 *Wapping* being prepared at Brighton Shed for its return under its own steam. Ralph Stent writes: '*This must be a first repaint as when first purchased in January 1905 for £700, the tank sides had* ROLVENDEN *sandwiched between the curved arcs of* ROTHER VALLEY *above and* RAILWAY *below*'.**

Plate 76 : **Ralph Stent writes: '*Awaiting works in Brighton Yard (No. 6 was the dead road), probably soon after April 1900*' (confirmed by Wilfred Palmer, as No. 325 *Abergavenny* re-entered traffic on 8th August that year). In a rear road is a glimpse of 'E4' Class No. 498 *Strettington*. No. 325 has the ordinary two panel lined tender with which it was suddenly withdrawn in 1909. The 'G' Class Single was a Tunbridge Wells engine from 1900 until the day Marsh travelled behind it. No. 325 lost time in driving rain, and he promptly out of hand called in the class, many members of which languished for years at Horsted Keynes, never to run again.**

Plate 77 : **'D' Class tank No. 33 *Mitcham* on the turntable alongside Brighton Shed with the imposing chalk cliff face mentioned on page 58. Ralph Stent comments: '*Returning from a trial trip, after repainting. This would have been at the end of May 1905, its last visit to shops and retaining its name*'. Its earliest years were spent at Epsom, but in 1897 it moved up to New Cross and became the spare engine to cover the many 'D' Class tanks stationed there.**

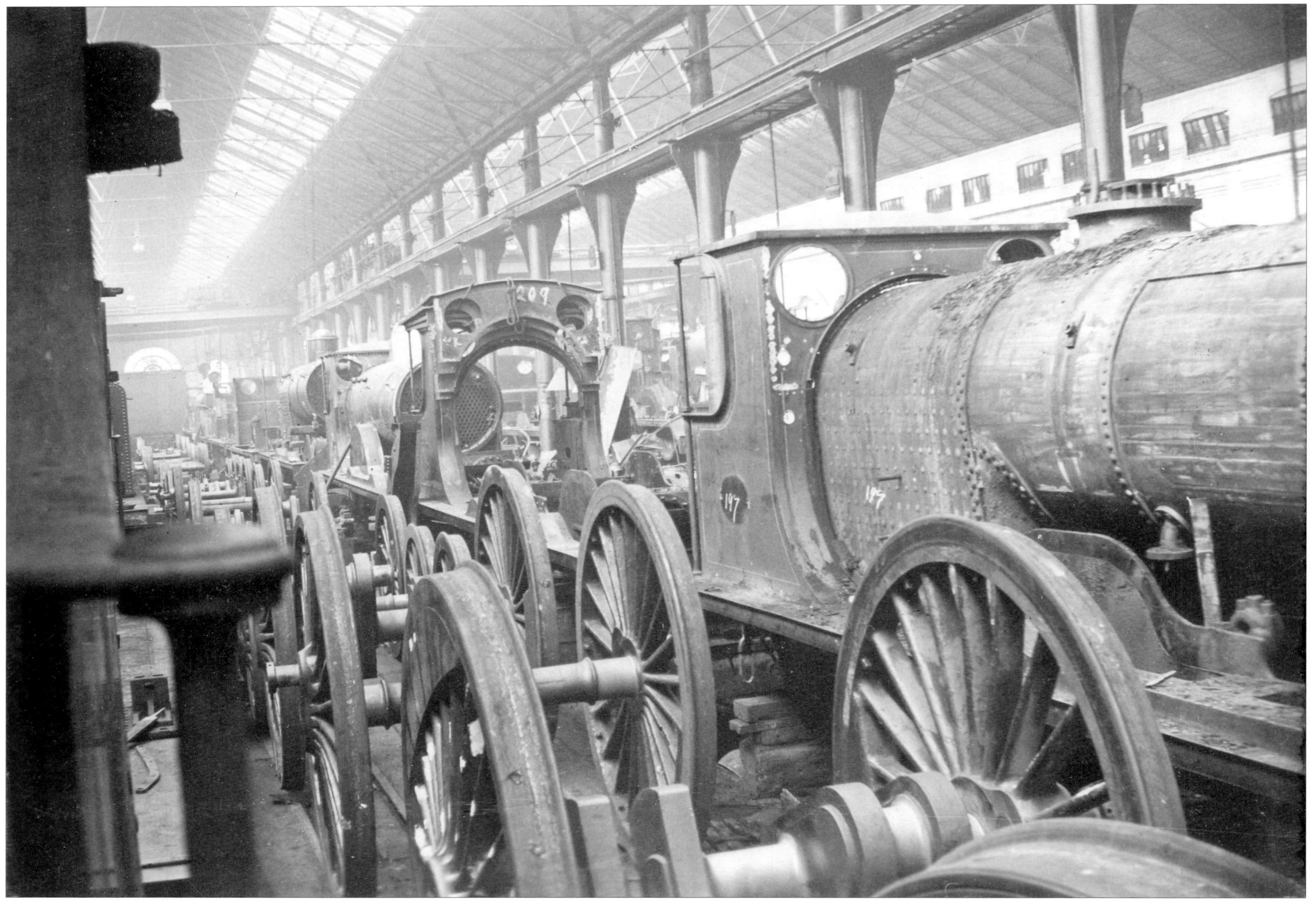

Plate 78 : **Inside the Erecting Shop at Brighton Works with 'Gladstone' No. 197 *Jonas Levy* followed by B2 No. 209 *Wolfe Barry*. Sadly the far end of the shop is somewhat faded but, prominent between the lines of locomotives, stands a most impressive array of wheels. Both engines were in for overhaul during the winter of 1905/6.**

Plate 79 : **Two of Marsh's new Atlantics receive attention in the Erecting Shop. The five 'H1's were delivered new from Kitsons between December 1905 and February 1906, slick work on behalf of a company desperate for heavier motive power. The photograph probably portrays their first major overhaul at Brighton. The date could well be 1910 when No. 189 *Edward Blount*, the 1889 Gold Medallist, lost its name when painted in Marsh umber livery.**

Above: Plate 80 : **'Gladstone' No. 189 *Edward Blount* was chosen by Marsh for a series of trials with Hammond's Patent Air-heating apparatus and entered the Erecting Shop on 23rd May 1907. A completely new smoke box was provided, divided into two compartments linked to two wings or pockets on either side. Emerging on the last day of November, the maker's claim of 15 to 20% fuel saving proved unfounded, mainly due to heat losses between smoke box and firebox. The apparatus was disconnected, although not removed from the engine, which eventually went for scrap in December 1912.**

Left: Plate 81 : **'D' Class tank No. 27 *Uckfield* inside the back of Brighton Works in April 1907, undergoing a major repair, and losing its name to emerge in the new Marsh umber livery. Engines of this class going through shops at this period were fitted with a new steel boiler to replace the Stroudley one which had been in use, in some cases, since 1873, and often for more than 700,000 running miles. Back in 1886 No. 27 had been the subject of a shortlived experiment, being fitted with Tarbutt's oil burning equipment. Next to it stands 'E1' Class No. 110 *Burgundy*, which survives today on the East Somerset Railway.**

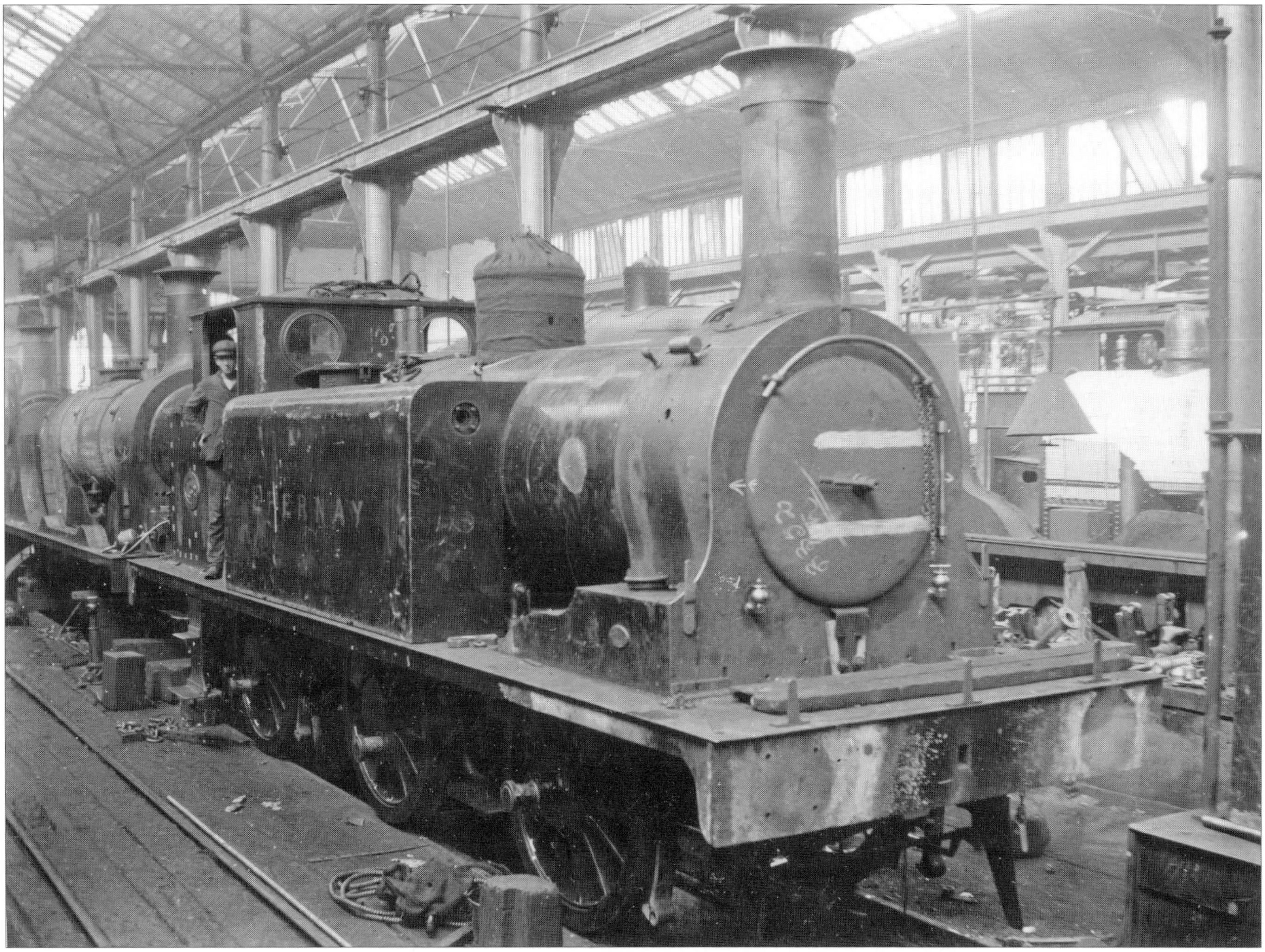

Plate 82 : **The 'E1' Class 0-6-0Ts were humble workhorses, giving good value service over many years. Though withdrawals commenced in 1908, the final survivor lasted until July 1961, even outlasting Maunsell's 'E1R' Class 0-6-2T rebuilds. No. 132 *Epernay* is seen in the Erecting Shop at Brighton early in 1908 when its Stroudley goods green livery seen here gave way to black with red lining and with the LB&SCR's initials on the tank sides. It lasted until 1926.**

Plate 83 : **The presence of the photographer provided a welcome break from the strict works regime, together with the opportunity to have this picture taken. The locomotive is 'Terrier' No. 662, about to part with its name *Martello*, and will leave Brighton works in 1909 in the new Marsh umber livery. Note the newly fitted coal rails introduced by Marsh. *Martello* is preserved today at the Bressingham Railway Museum, Diss, and is presently in working order and has paid visits to several heritage railways.**

Plate 84 : **The final 'D' Class tank No. 362 *Kidbrooke* which first entered service in March 1887. It carries the unusual combination of a Marsh boiler and a Stroudley name, which it was to lose after this 1909 overhaul. As can be seen on the front buffer beam, it was an Eastbourne engine, and just managed to make its fortieth year before being withdrawn in October 1927.**

Plate 85 : **This corner of Brighton Works shows a set of drilling machines used in the manufacture of tube plates. A large number of such pictures appear in the Oakwood Press biography of Douglas Earle Marsh and later formed part of the well known Richardson collection.**

courtesy Lawrence Marshall collection

Plate 86 : **The large number of photographs taken in the works does seem to point to one of Henry Bennett's boys being briefly employed there. So many photographs showing Walter amongst the locomotives in the works (See introductory section) points to these probably being taken either by his father or by his brother Maurice. This photograph, taken in the Boiler Shop, shows boiler barrels and backplates under construction.** ***courtesy Lawrence Marshall collection***

Plate 87 : **Back outside the works Stroudley 'C1' Class Jumbo No. 427 stands out in Brighton Works yard, possibly on 7th December 1904, the day it entered the Erecting Shop, judging by the clean works shunter seen behind. Note the number plate in this print is covered with white preserving compound, which denoted that the engine was in for heavy repairs, not scrapping. In fact the 1884 built locomotive was only finally withdrawn in March 1911. To the right is the tender of No. 206 (*below*); these two engines were known to be in shops together at that time.**

Plate 88 : **Ralph Stent writes: '*Rough ex-shops in Brighton yard in January 1909. 'B2' Class No. 206 (formerly* Smeaton*) has been converted to Class 'B2x' with 'C3' pattern boiler and extended smokebox supported by a saddle, and a spacious cab which overlapped the trailing splashers*'. Note the works date plate has been removed from the splasher to the running frame. Later still in 1921 it was fitted with a top feed double-domed boiler.**

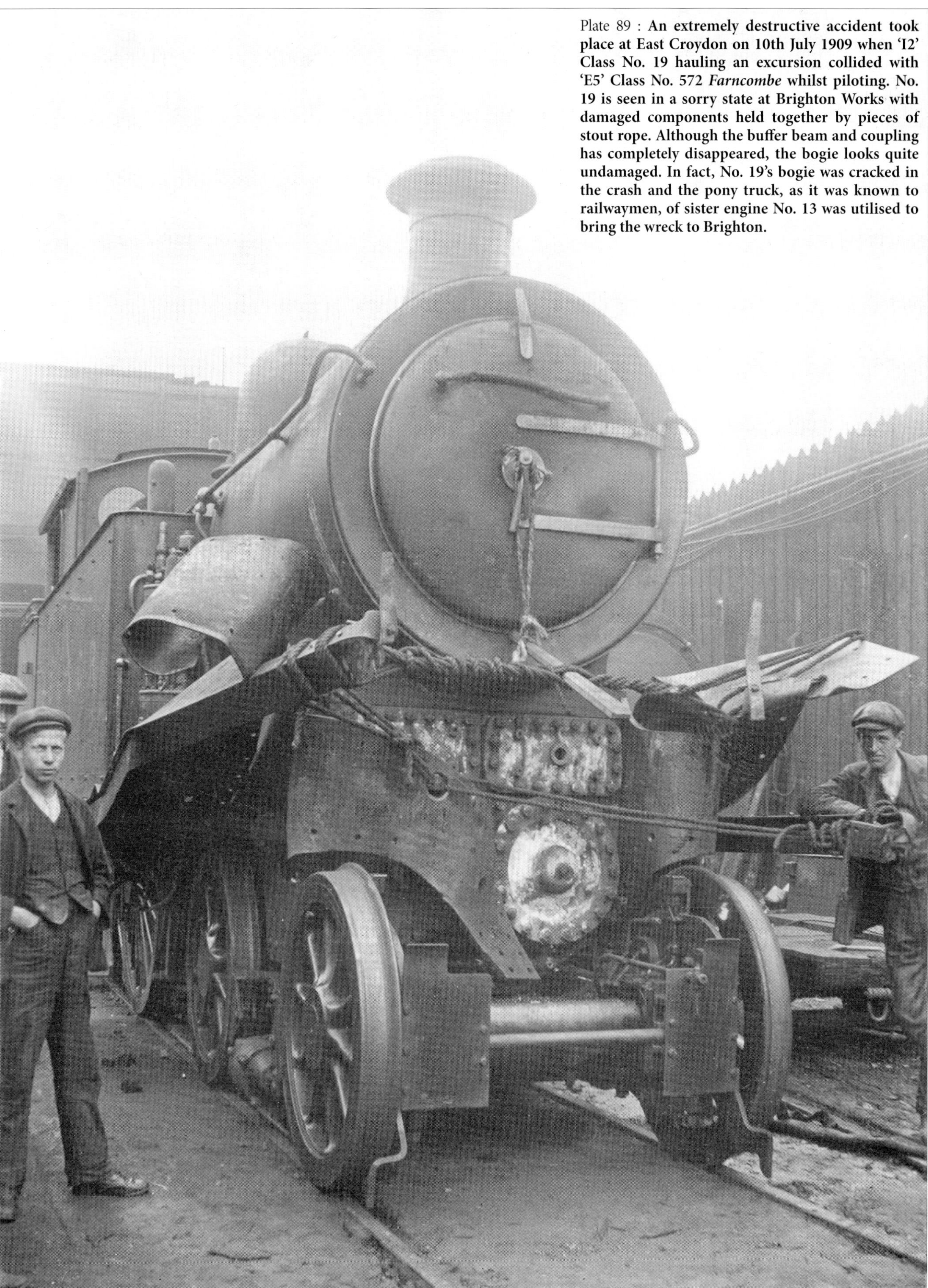

Plate 89 : **An extremely destructive accident took place at East Croydon on 10th July 1909 when 'I2' Class No. 19 hauling an excursion collided with 'E5' Class No. 572 *Farncombe* whilst piloting. No. 19 is seen in a sorry state at Brighton Works with damaged components held together by pieces of stout rope. Although the buffer beam and coupling has completely disappeared, the bogie looks quite undamaged. In fact, No. 19's bogie was cracked in the crash and the pony truck, as it was known to railwaymen, of sister engine No. 13 was utilised to bring the wreck to Brighton.**

Plate 90 : **If there are so many portraits of 'D' Class tanks, it was because they were the most numerous class on the system, quite apart from being a delightful design. No. 236 *Ardingly* stands outside the Erecting Shop in 1908. Its driver over the previous decade was Charles J. Broadbridge and the locomotive was based at Horsham shed. Note the blast pipe stood on the front buffer beam.**

Plate 91 : **Brand new rebuilt 'D3x' Class No. 397 stands at the back of Brighton Works in June 1907. It carries a larger boiler of Marsh design with an extended smoke box carried on a saddle. Financial constraints led Marsh to use two spare 'I2' Class boilers on a pair of 'D3's, but this experiment met with limited success, for performance was not improved. Not well received by locomotive crews, they both went before their time, No. 397 in July 1948.**

Plate 92: **Another rare picture, unusual in that it provides a glimpse on the extreme left of the turntable within Brighton Works yard with B4 No. 68 *Marlborough* about to be turned there rather than on the table at Brighton shed. No. 68, a Battersea Engine, may well have arrived under its own steam to be turned before entering shops as all engines in the Erecting Shop faced south, which it did in May 1906 for transformation into Marsh umber. It still, however, has a tender topped high with coal. Intriguing!**

Plate 93 : 'G' Class Single No. 332 *Shanklin*, a Battersea engine, has its lamp and headcode changed by the fireman who has a word with his driver, Frederick Timmins, as they wait in a queue of engines in the centre of three roads between the platforms. Note the temporary platform awnings at the time of Victoria Station's reconstruction.

Plate 94 : **Between 1903 and 1907 Victoria Station was rebuilt, including doubling the platforms in length southwards over the remaining part of the Grosvenor Canal. One of the grand fluted capitals lies prone beside 'E3' Class 0-6-2T No. 169 *Bedhampton* in old Victoria. The new station opened on 10th February 1907. No. 169 entered Brighton works in August 1907 and re-entered traffic nameless in April 1908.**

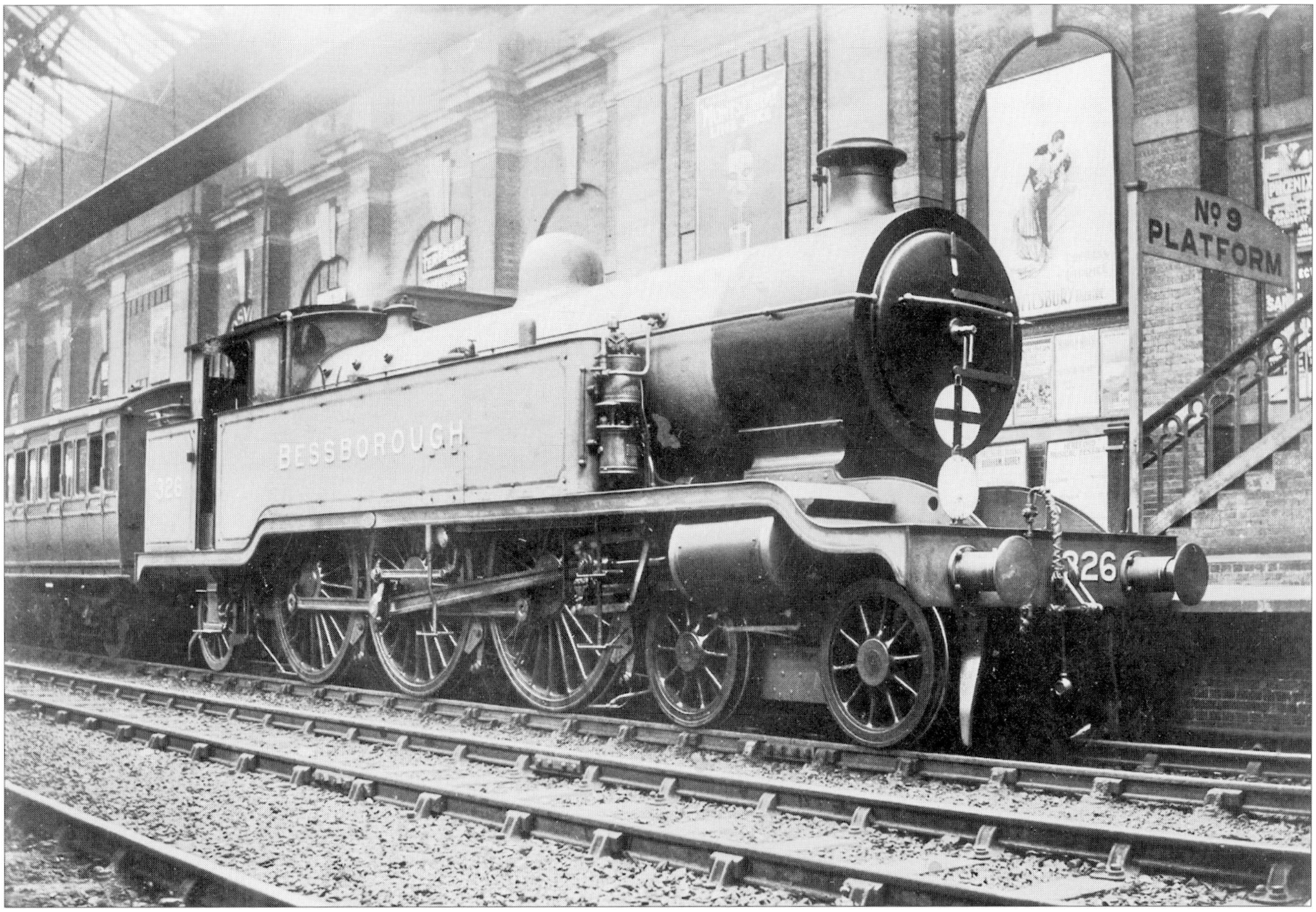

Plate 95 : **A late Bennett picture in the newly rebuilt Victoria Station. No. 9 Platform was the westernmost one with Buckingham Palace Road the other side of the platform wall. Marsh's 'J' Class 4-6-2T No. 326 *Bessborough*, still in works grey and facing the buffer stops, towers above the diminutive Billinton stock of its train which has arrived from Brighton, possibly with Walter Bennett on board.**

Plate 96 : **Another late Bennett picture showing No. 576, formerly named *Brenchley*, a Marsh 'E5x' rebuild of July 1911, here seen under the wires at the exit of Victoria Station. It was to survive until July 1955. Although the result was not an outstanding success, in terms of motive power the rebuilds just shaded their untouched 'E5' companions.**

Plate 97 : **A 'Gladstone' on a Down express, which includes a Pullman car, is captured from the north end of Battersea Park station, a rare view taken before the 1906-7 widening. Behind the locomotive is Battersea Park Junction signal box dating from 1865, and originally known as York Road Junction. To its left the roof of one of Battersea Shed's roundhouses is visible, and behind the fine gantry of Up starter signals lie the works of an early motor manufacturer or repairer, the Burlington Motor Car Co. Ltd.**

Plate 98 : **An early pre-1902 photograph of Stroudley 'Terrier' No. 40 *Brighton*, which spent its early LB&SCR career at Battersea Shed where Bennett took this portrait. Entering traffic in March 1878, it appears to have been so named in anticipation of the 1878 Paris Exhibition where it received a gold medal. It was sold to the Isle of Wight Central Railway in 1901 being delivered to the island on the 8th January following. In July/ August 1918 it was rebuilt to Class 'A1x', named *Newport* in June 1930, returned to the mainland in 1947 and was withdrawn in 1963. After display at Butlins holiday camp at Pwllheli it was returned ten years later to the Isle of Wight Steam Railway to be restored as IWC No. 11.**

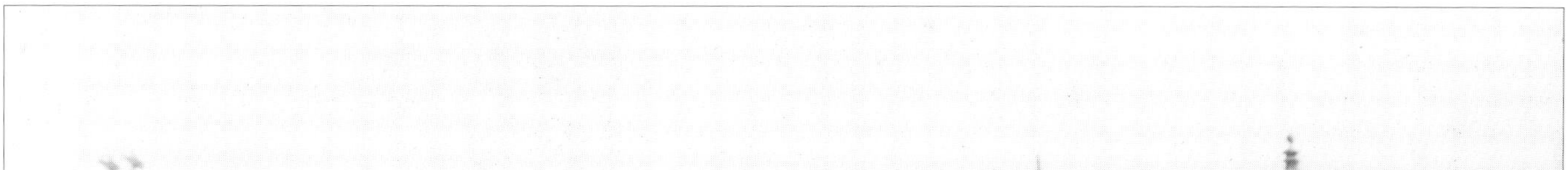

Plate 99 : **This informal portrait of Class 'E5' No. 593 *Hollington*, a resident of Battersea up till the end of World War One, was taken on a rare visit to Battersea depot. It was probably taken soon after the locomotive entered service in May 1904, judging from its pristine condition. Its driver was William Clarke, seen in the cab with his fireman, while cleaning staff in the foreground make for an unusual picture.**

Plate 100 : **This view shows the squeezed in Platform No. 7 at Clapham Junction accommodating the LB&SCR Up line. In Platform No. 8 a Stroudley 'D2' Class 0-4-2 on a down working for Hastings stands under the lengthy footbridge connecting the various platforms, which stops at the L&SWR Platform No. 6 from which the photograph has been taken. Platform No. 9 on the other side of the island platform was another Up line and beyond lay the West London Extension lines, the platform of which is just visible peeping through the station name board.**

Plate 101 : **The first LB&SCR station at Clapham Junction was opened on 2nd March 1863 at the same time as the WLER from Kensington, and used three tracks as far south as Balham. Bennett took his photograph of 'D' Class tank *Pelham* just below the footbridge visible in the previous picture, prior to the 1907-8 rebuilding. Additional land was obtained for this by the acquisition and demolition of various properties adjacent to the south side and necessitating the slewing of the WLER tracks to leave room for re-arrangements to accommodate the fourth track as part of the main line widening from Victoria through to just north of Balcombe Tunnel.**

Plate 102 : **A 'B2' Class 4-4-0 brings an Up working into Clapham Junction. The South box, seen towering above St. John's Hill bridge was erected in 1892, and under the SR was known as C box. At this time the L&SWR main line was still just a double track. On the left the retaining wall of the LB&SCR's cab road to its rather grand station frontage, built in the winter of 1873-4, is bedecked with a continuous line of advertisement hoardings.**

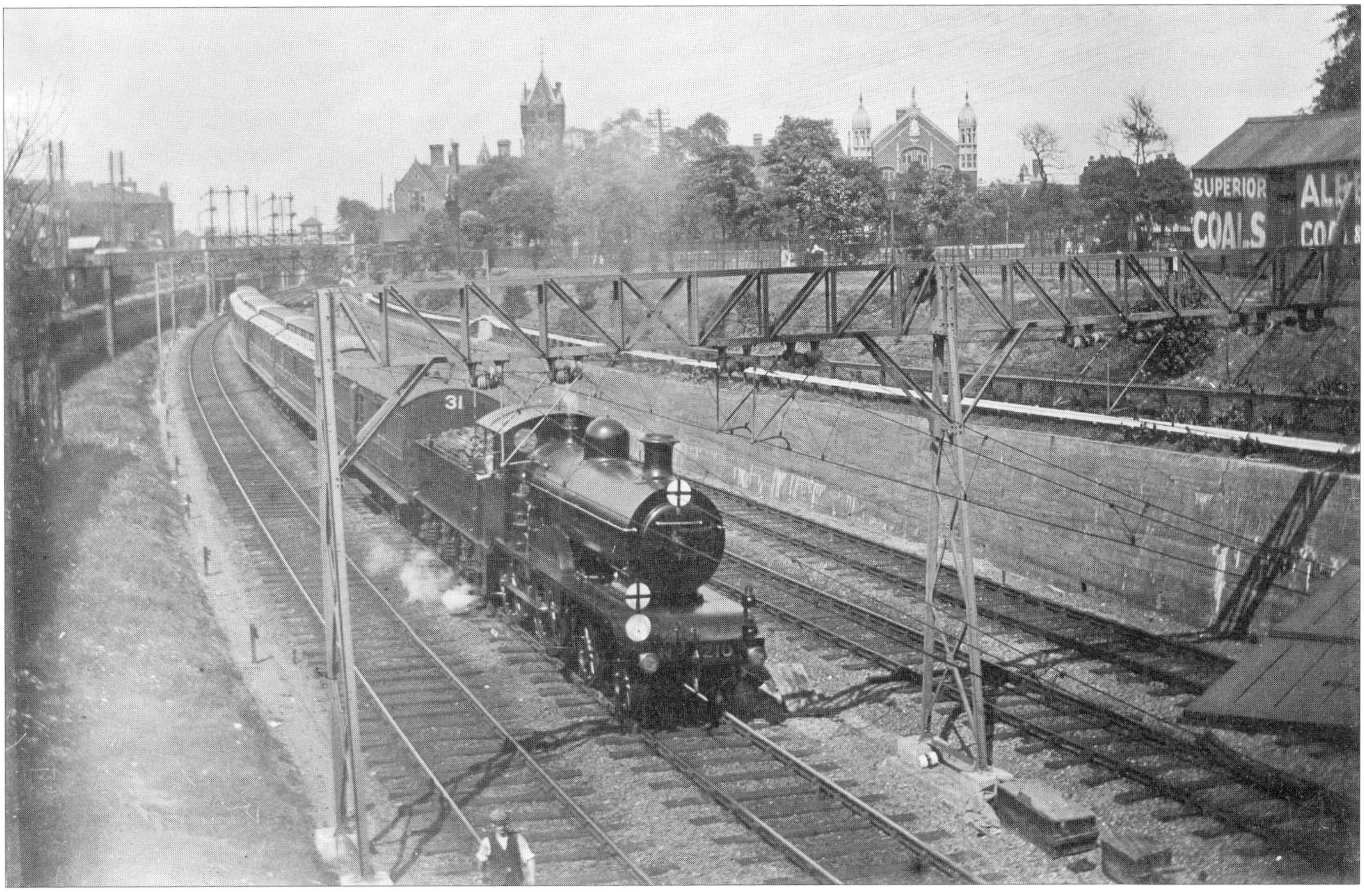

Plate 103 : **From about 1910 Walter Bennett seems to have taken up photography in his own right. Taken from the road bridge carrying Battersea Rise over both the L&SWR lines (left) and those of the LB&SCR, 'B2x' Class No. 210 (formerly *Fairbairn*), rebuilt by Marsh in February 1909, takes the curve out of Clapham Junction under the wires with an express of clerestory carriages bound for Brighton. The Superior Coals tin shed has long since vanished and today a footpath overlooking the railway links Battersea Rise to Strath Terrace, the next bridge, and on to St. John's Hill. On the reverse is inscribed: '*Our reporting place*', indicating the popularity of this viewpoint for photographers and trainspotters.**

Plate 104: 'D' Class No. 251 *Singleton*, a Battersea engine and later, as here, a Horsham one, is seen at Mitcham Junction. It went through works between November 1904 and September 1905, an extremely long overhaul, but early enough in Marsh's regime to retain its name before the new livery had been decided upon. Here the locomotive has been beautifully cleaned and makes a splendid picture.

Plate 105 : **Entering Epsom on a Victoria-Portsmouth stopping train in the spring of 1909, 'E5' Class No. 575 *Westergate*, passes a Class 'D' tank waiting with the stock of a returning local to the capital. The 'E5' is running as a 2-4-2T, being one of twenty converted by Marsh from 0-6-2T by removal of the leading coupling rod sections. Marsh had arrived from Doncaster with an acute aversion towards using front-coupled tank engines on secondary services. By September 1909, however, all twenty had reverted to their former wheel arrangement.**

Plate 106 : **'D' Class tanks No's 264 *Langston* and 285 *Holmwood* stand back to back outside Epsom Shed. Both engines were based there for suburban work in the mid-Edwardian period. The shed was located at the north end of No. 1 platform at Epsom Town LB&SC station and closed when electric services arrived in March 1929.**

Plate 107 : **Class 'D' tank No. 295 (formerly *Whippingham*) of Epsom Shed stands in the platform of the LB&SCR's Town station. Still with name and Stroudley livery, it spent a short time in store at Horsted Keynes in the early months of 1906. It then went into Brighton works and emerged as seen above on 7th November that year, nameless and in Marsh umber livery. Both station and the small two road engine shed closed in March 1929. The Waterloo services had been electrified the previous year and a new and modern station constructed to replace the separate LB&SCR and L&SWR stations. Goods traffic, however, was retained at the former LB&SCR station and part of the large goods shed can be seen to the left of No. 295.**

Plate 108 : **Brighton 'Grasshopper' 4-4-0 No. 203 (late *Henry Fletcher*) enters Ashtead L&SWR station on the section between Epsom and Leatherhead over which the LB&SCR had running rights. This locomotive assumed Marsh umber livery in July 1906, which means the photograph was taken after this date, probably soon after judging by the glistening condition of the locomotive.**

Plate 109 : **Marsh Atlantic No. 40, under the charge of Driver George Pont of Brighton shed, approaches Boxhill & Burford Bridge Station and the start of the tell-tale hedgerow with an express for Portsmouth via Mitcham, Sutton, Epsom, Dorking and Horsham composed of two-tone elliptical stock. The Company just could not make up its mind, as with several others on the system, over the appropriate name of the station which started as West Humble until 1870, Boxhill & Burford Bridge until 1896, plain Boxhill until 1904, then Boxhill & Burford Bridge again. Today it is Boxhill & Westhumble!**

Plate 110 : **Dorking and surrounds comes in for an unusual proportion of Bennett pictures. Possibly the family may have had friends or relatives in the area giving cause for frequent visits. Here we see 'D' Class tank No. 265 (formerly *Chipstead*) approaching Boxhill & Burford Bridge Station with the neat hedge and path embracing the cutting and taking the rising slope up to the road bridge. No. 265 was a Horsham engine and the photograph must have been taken after April 1906. One must be grateful at least to Marsh for placing the loco number on the front buffer beam, or else one would be unable to identify the locomotives for picture captions.**

Plate 111 : **This photograph is taken the other way looking south. The train, having just passed under the road bridge leading to the station and heading for London, originating from Littlehampton via Horsham, where it would in all likelihood have filled up its water tanks. 'D' Class No. 355 (formerly *Worthing*) was a New Cross engine and an early conversion to the new Marsh livery in March 1906.**

Plate 112 : **Class 'D' tank No. 291 *Deepdene* leaves Dorking with plenty of steam to spare as it sets out for London with a train comprising a close-coupled suburban set, one of twenty built between 1898 and 1901, under the eyes of the signalman high up in the 31 lever North box erected in 1877, and in use until March 1938. The tall box gave a clear view over the west side carriage sidings, goods and loco yards and also enabled the signalman to see over the London Road bridge from which the picture was taken. To his credit Bennett took the trouble to note on the reverse: '*E4 No. 467* Berwick *(Battersea) under the tall signal; D No. 298* Southwark *(New Cross) behind No. 467's train, and E1s No. 86* Geneva *(New Cross) and No. 90* Berne *(Battersea)*'. The amount of smoke over the area must frequently have been a problem for the signalman.**

Plate 113 : **'D' Class tank No. 229 *Dorking*, with the driver trimming the coal, at Dorking in the east side carriage sidings with the rising slopes of Boxhill in the right background. In spite of those naive people who imagined the engine name to represent the destination, there was a distinct policy on the system of allocating the town and village names of locomotives to depots in their local area. Thus Dorking shed not only had its namesake but also *Deepdene*, *Denbies*, *Effingham* and *Holmbury*. When nearly all the names disappeared under Marsh, this policy no longer pertained and locomotives were allocated as convenient to the Locomotive Department.**

Plate 114 : **Class 'D' tank *Belmont* renumbered to 619 in the scheme to make number series space for Marsh's 'I' Class Atlantic tank engines, stands in a group of fellow class members next to No. 229 *Dorking* and No. 289 *Holmbury* parked in the shed area. The shed was blown down around the turn of the century and thereafter locomotives stood out in the open. In the background stands the frontage of the imposing station house designed by Charles H. Driver which was approached up a wide avenue.**

Plate 115 : **Another non-Dorking named 'D' Class tank No. 259 (formerly *Barnham*) stands on the site of Dorking shed in company with fellow class members. Named *Telford* until April 1898, this New Cross engine went through Brighton works in 1907 to receive the livery shown here. The grass foreground and adjacent trees testify to what a rural shed Dorking was. It finally closed in 1929 when electric services reached the town.**

Plate 116 : **'B2' Class No. 204, which took the name *Telford* from No. 259 seen above, tackles the 1 in 90 gradient out of Dorking towards Deepdene and the final ridge of the North Downs c1910. At this stage it was stationed at Horsham under Driver Seymour Apps. It is at the point of running over the junction of the former spur to the Guildford-Redhill line. This was retained as siding until about 1926, the unused land thereabouts being used for storage of hay collected from the lineside elsewhere and used to feed the Company's numerous cartage and shunting horses.**

Plate 117 : **One of the few Horsham photographs in the Bennett collection epitomises all that the LB&SCR stood for! Immaculate 'D' Class tank No. 270, taken soon after return from works in 1905, gleams in the sunshine. The open rural vista beyond Horsham shed, where *Warnham* was based, is seen before local industry began to hem in the site.**

Plate 118 : **A well taken photograph of 'B2' Class 4-4-0 No. 204, taken near West Horsham, today Christ's Hospital. The headcode indicates a working between Victoria, Mitcham, Sutton, Epsom, Leatherhead, Dorking, Horsham and Portsmouth. No. 204 went through shops in the spring of 1906 to receive Marsh umber. The earliest date this picture could have been taken must have been 7th March 1906 when it re-entered traffic.**

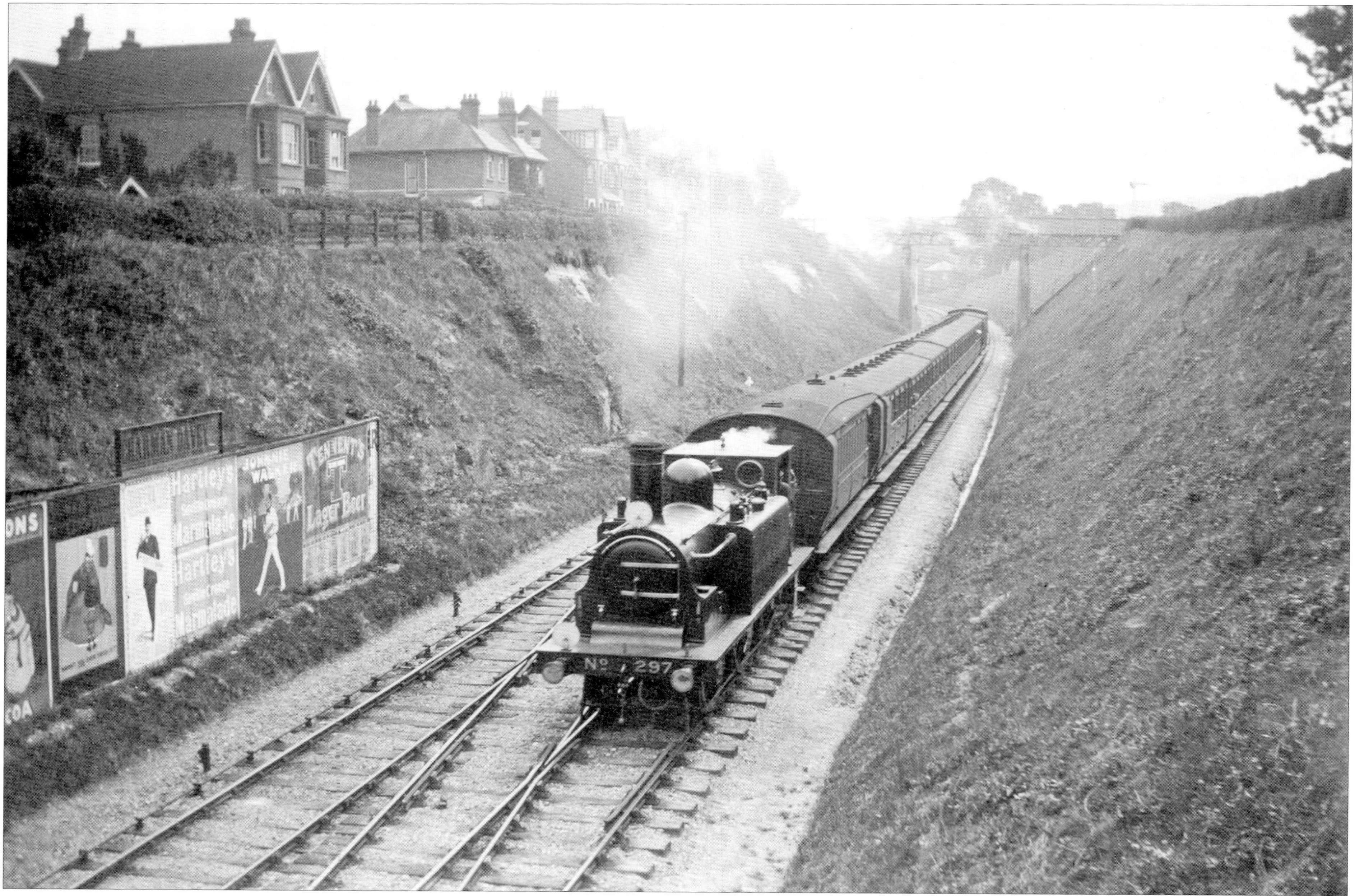

Plate 119 : **Yet another 'D', No. 297 (old *Bonchurch*) captured in the cutting approaching Steyning Station from the south. It had resumed passenger duties in 1906 following a spell as Paint Shop pilot and assuming Marsh livery on going through works in December 1908. The train consists of Stroudley four-wheelers except for the leading Billinton luggage van. It is passing an 'Advertising Station' run by Charman Davey, placed here in the most rural of locations. Charman Davey were a leading firm of advertising contractors with several such stations on the LB&SC. Most of the products advertised like Tennents lager beer, Johnnie Walker whisky and Hartley's marmalade show products have not changed all that much in the meantime.**

Plate 120 : **'D3' Class 0-4-4Ts came to monopolise the Steyning line services in the post-Grouping years but here is No. 373 (formerly *Billingshurst*) rounding a curve out of Bramber Station with a train in the Horsham direction. It is worth noting the neat appearance of the permanent way and the grass verges of those distant days. No. 373 lost its name in 1909.**

Plate 121 : **No. 596, the pioneer 'I1' Class Atlantic tank which emerged from Brighton Works in September 1906, based largely on H. A. Ivatt's 'C12' Class 4-4-2Ts of 1898, enters Bramber from the south. The first two had straight-sided smoke boxes, tapered boilers and roof-top clerestories with adjustable ventilating louvres. No. 595, as can be seen, carried a modified 'E5' Class chimney.**

Plate 122 : **The scene is Portsmouth Harbour station with 'B2' Class No. 318 *Rothschild* in charge of an eastbound working. As with many of the 'B2's, it was a Portsmouth engine based at Fratton Shed from which the class worked up quite a mileage. No. 318, for instance, between shoppings at Brighton ran 91,975 miles from 13th October 1904 until 18th October 1906. After overhaul it emerged without its name near the end of March 1907. The almost horizontal smoke leaving the chimney indicates a fairly strong wind; in fact on 12th December 1893 a sudden gale caused the collapse of a large part of the station awnings.**

Plate 123 : **This was the kind of picture that sold well in the Bennett photographic list, and a royal engine with all its decorative panoply was just the thing to improve the sales. Engines on Royal Specials to Portsmouth Dockyard would have been coaled and watered at Fratton, where this great portrait of Marsh Atlantic No. 40 was taken. The insignia on view includes the special royal headlamps, the headcode discs bearing the crown, the crown hung from the top of the lamp bracket, the coat of arms itself and that between the two splashers. Much of this was preserved in the proposed Eastleigh Works museum under SR auspices and has survived to this day at the National Railway Museum.** ***courtesy Lawrence Marshall collection***

Plate 124 : **A view like this has often been confused with the terrain on the Crumbles ballast line at Eastbourne, but this is at Fratton, a joint engine shed with the L&SWR. In 1891 it was decided to replace the original four road shed near the Town station with a square roundhouse with separate coaling facilities for each company, and each had separate stalls within the shed. When first built it lay on the edge of Portsmouth in open countryside, hence the open aspect. 'B2' Class No. 317 *Gerald Loder* receives an oil round before proceeding on its next assignment. By Edwardian days the 'B2's had ousted the 'G' Class 2-2-2s from their former monopoly of the Portsmouth services.**

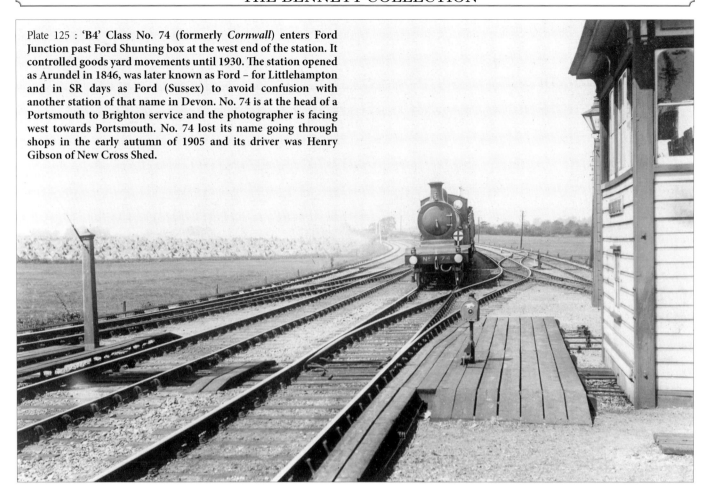

Plate 125 : **'B4' Class No. 74 (formerly *Cornwall*) enters Ford Junction past Ford Shunting box at the west end of the station. It controlled goods yard movements until 1930. The station opened as Arundel in 1846, was later known as Ford – for Littlehampton and in SR days as Ford (Sussex) to avoid confusion with another station of that name in Devon. No. 74 is at the head of a Portsmouth to Brighton service and the photographer is facing west towards Portsmouth. No. 74 lost its name going through shops in the early autumn of 1905 and its driver was Henry Gibson of New Cross Shed.**

Plate 126 : **The photograph has written on reverse: '*Replacing* Hartfield *(D tank No. 26) on the line*' at Ford Junction'. No. 26 is being lifted by one of the LB&SCR's breakdown cranes supplied in 1898. So far any details of this incident have not come to light, but if this was a goods working and there was no loss of life or serious injury, it might not have been worth reporting. A derailment in the bay platform road would have caused minimal disruption to traffic. Faintly visible in the distance is the old Ford station East signal box that, according to the records dated from 1875, but to judge from its appearance may have been a 1860s box moved from another location. It was replaced on 30th September 1930.**

Plate 127 : **Another Bennett gem, taken at the West Worthing end of the motor train service from Brighton, and especially interesting because of Marsh's experimental conversion to the unusual 2-4-0 wheel arrangement, being handed over, following some teething problems, to the Running Department on 18th July 1905. Its locomotive crew from that time was Driver Henry Lewry and Fireman William Sands. It was the 'Terrier' selected for the National Collection, still in A1 condition, being withdrawn in August 1946, living in sheds in various corners of the kingdom and being displayed at the 1948 Waterloo Centenary and Eastleigh Works Open days before going to the BTC's Clapham transport Museum and on to the NRM at York.**

courtesy Lawrence Marshall collection

Plate 128 : **No. 643, the former 'Terrier' oddly named** ***Gipsyhill*****, stands at Worthing on rail motor service. It acquired its Marsh livery in May 1906. Ralph Stent notes on reverse:: '*Tom Hatcher (formerly driver of No. 82* Boxhill *peeping through the front end*'. This is confirmed by Wilfred Palmer recording in his notebook 'Thomas Hatcher' who shared the engine with George Reeves, both crew and locomotive belonging to Brighton Shed'.**

Plate 129: **An unidentified 'D' Class tank sporting a replacement Billinton boiler and its immaculate gamboge livery leaves behind the houses of Portslade and is approaching a footbridge near Fishergate from which Henry Bennett is taking the picture. The seven coach set is of Billinton stock and every detail of the train has been picked out crystal clear in the coastal sunshine. Allotments, market gardens and ploughed fields recapture an idyllic scene that sadly is no more. Fishersgate Halt was opened in 1905, obliterating the railwaymen's allotments at this point.**

Plate 130 : **Rather nearer to Portslade, the station of which can just be seen in the distance, Class 'D3' No. 381 *Fittleworth*, still glistening in Stroudley gamboge, heads a local of mixed Stroudley and Billinton stock along the flat coastal plain. While the area is still largely rural, housing developments are already covering the fields on the coastal side, and by the First World War most of the land as far west as Shoreham was built up.**

Plate 131 : **Stroudley 'Terrier' No. 79 (*Minories* no longer under the Marsh regime) with Balloon on the Worthing to Brighton all halts, entering Dyke Junction c1910. The Dyke branch is seen leaving the main coastal line on the right. The 1910 timetable showed eleven rail motor workings to Worthing, five of which were extended to West Worthing. The junction halt, opened on 15th September 1905, was renamed Aldrington in 1932, though one rail atlas has it as Devil's Dyke Halt!**

Plate 132 : **Taken the same day, this time a westbound working to Worthing, providing a view of the halt and in the distance Dyke Junction signal box. This was one of a set of small halts specially introduced for the motor trains, the others being at Holland Road and Ham Bridge, later East Worthing (3rd September 1905), Fishergate (15th September 1905). Bungalow Town, just west of Shoreham viaduct and which was later renamed Shoreham Airport, was opened in 1910.**

Plate 133 : **A Brighton bound service from the Dyke is held at the signal at the approach to the main line at Dyke Junction on 1st August 1907. Motive power is unusual in that 'E1' Class goods tank No. 122 *Leghorn* is in charge. It was a New Cross based locomotive and could well have been used by Brighton Shed to fill in while awaiting works. It returned to traffic in Marsh goods black in October that year. It was fellow class member No. 101 *Orleans* that hauled the inaugural train out of Brighton Station at noon on 1st September 1887. In spite of stops introduced to serve the Brighton & Hove Golf Club and at Rowan Halt to tap the latest suburban development, falling traffic spelt its doom and the final train ran on the last day of 1938.**

Plate 134 : **Despite the seemingly bleak conditions that frequently obtained at the Dyke, Henry Bennett was not deterred from recording the train guard in full regalia with straps and polished clasps and badges, posing with his little boy (also displaying brass buttons!) beside the smoke box of 'E4' Class No. 484 *Hackbridge*. An 'E4' at this early date, c1907, is unusual at the Dyke, the Edwardian services being very much in the hands of the 'D' Class tanks and the occasional 'E1' 0-6-0T. The figure holding the glass plates near the platform lamp post is Maurice Bennett, well into his teens. The low light has caught the wheels and motion of *Hackbridge* to perfection.**

Plate 135 : **The classic motor train, a delightful combination of 'Terrier' and Balloon coach on the service to Worthing, having just passed under Olive Road bridge, close to Aldrington Farm. The locomotive is No. 81 (ex *Beulah*), converted by Marsh to run as a 2-4-0T on the new coastal service calling at the several new halts constructed to offer a frequent and convenient service to the coastal belt west of Brighton. The economical workings spread to other parts of the Brighton's system, including London suburbia in an effort to challenge the competition of the new trams.**

Plate 136 : **Another Brighton bound service from the Dyke passes on to the main line at Dyke Junction. It was some years before some of the more powerful 'D' Class tanks were fitted with motor train equipment as loads increased on these services, but the occasional unavailability of an engine resulted in a 'D' standing in on these duties. Here No. 223 *Balcombe* stands at Dyke Junction Halt c1908 and is about to enter a more industrial landscape as it proceeds towards Brighton. From May 1904 No. 223 is noted as Spare engine based at Brighton Shed.**

Plate 137 : **Scarcely a mile out of Hove, and not a building in sight amidst the wide open undeveloped fields. The scene is the shallow cutting beyond Aldrington with the cemetery enclosed by trees on the skyline. This photograph was another Henry Bennett coup, catching brand new 'C3' Class No. 303 on a trial trip along the coast line. Note the Special and Worthing headcode, the former status denoted by the double diamond disc at the top of the smoke box, and also that the locomotive is stopped for smokebox inspection.**

Plate 138 : **Once again the same setting, a favourite for the Bennetts, as 'Gladstone' No. 196 *Ralph L Lopes* in charge of a delightful short train with a passenger brake van at rear. It was a Bognor based engine in the early Edwardian period but was in Brighton Works from 19th November 1906 to 30th January 1907 to emerge nameless in Marsh umber livery.**

Plate 139 : **Photographed around 1906 without its name *Godalming*, which it lost in October 1905, 'E4' Class No. 486 seeks to speed up a westbound goods on this heavily utilised section up to Shoreham. It includes four goods brakes, the first three to Stroudley design, and a variety of wagons, several of them sheeted over their bars in true LB&SCR fashion. Prior to receiving its umber livery, it was experimentally painted in glossy black with red and white lining to present to the Directors when Marsh was investigating a new and less expensive livery.**

Plate 140 : **A Billinton 'C2' Class 0-6-0 trundles its goods train westwards through the industrial surroundings of west Hove. No. 440 was a Brighton engine through and through, having been based there from the outset when it first entered traffic in May 1893. It entered works in October 1906, and is seen here in Marsh lined black goods livery. Marsh transformed this underpowered class by fitting his two-ring 5ft modified boiler onto the 'C2' chassis, resulting in an enhanced performance. No. 440 was so rebuilt in December 1911. Again there are a number of brake vans on the front of the train, this time two Billinton vans with a Stroudley example in between.**

Plate 141 : **A couple of hundred yards further on with the same signals now in the distance, No. 9, still in mint condition after entering traffic in December 1907, looks out of place at the front of a lengthy train of the previous generation's coaching stock. Behind the imposing lamp post a 'D3' Class 0-4-4T stands in as a yard shunter in Hove West yard, and to the right are three private owner wagons including Price & Company and Wm Colwell both based in Hove. On the skyline is Parsons & Sons factory.**

Plate 142 : **Marsh's first design of tank locomotive, the 'I1' Class, was unsuccessful, mainly because of the very small boiler, and led to many complaints by the engine crews, particularly over ventilation since the side tanks encroached into the cab. Here No. 3 hauls a local comprising four Billinton six-wheelers in the two tone livery into Hove from the west past some of the usual goods opens and a Stroudley brake, No. 137, the steps of which are whitened for safety reasons.**

Plate 143 : **With Hove station in the background, ‘I2’ Class No. 15 heads away westwards towards Portsmouth. Entering service in May 1908, this Battersea locomotive driven by George Duffin has brought the train from Victoria via the Cliftonville curve, and had been used as a Royal Train locomotive to bring King Edward VII to the Derby at Epsom Downs on the 15th of that same month.**

Plate 144 : **Same headcode but an earlier date as veteran ‘Single’ No. 325 *Abergavenny* of Tunbridge Wells Shed takes a westbound working along the south coast main line to Portsmouth. A pre-1909 photograph, the date when No. 325 was withdrawn at a stroke by an irate Marsh (see picture page 61).**

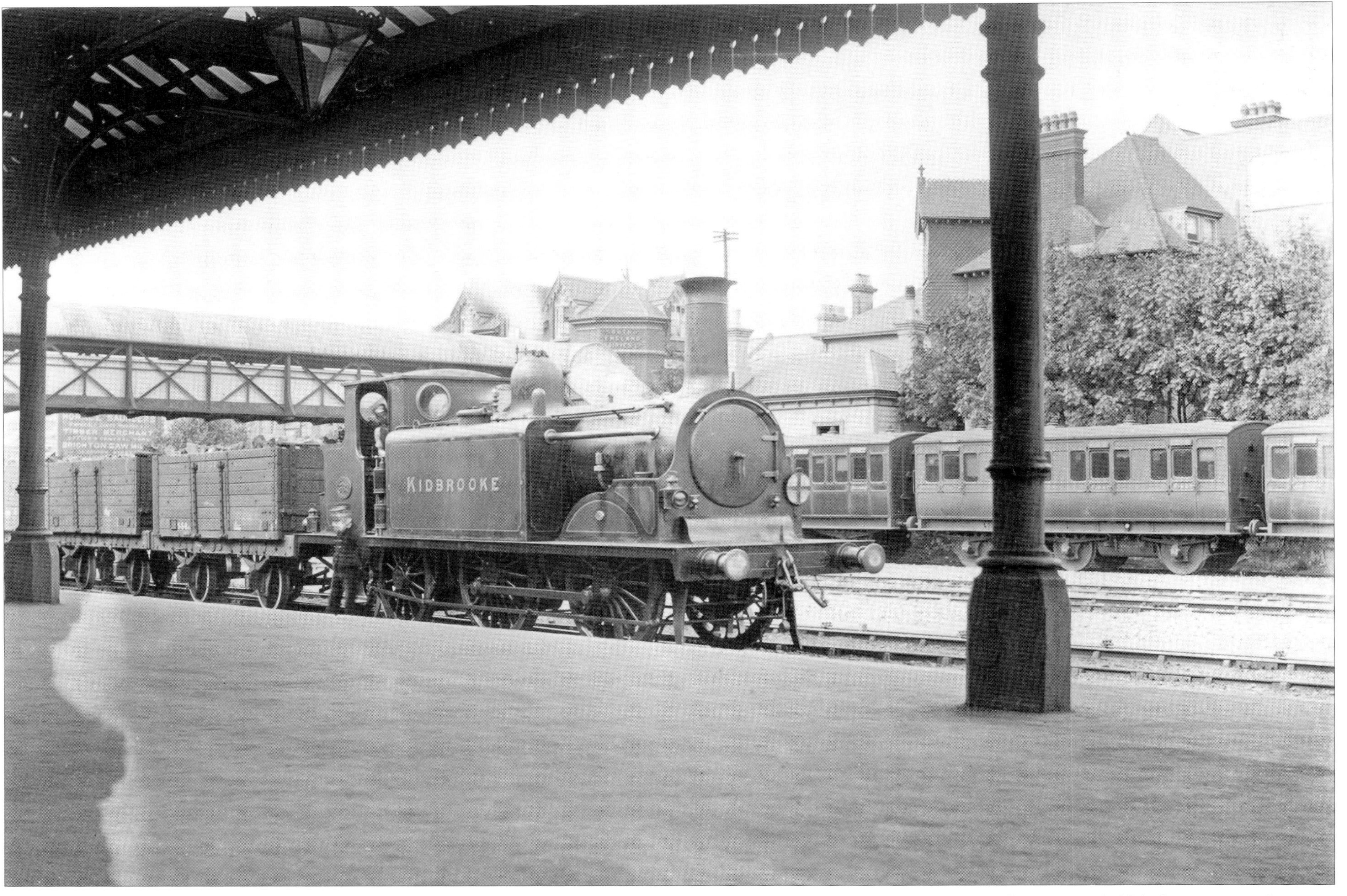

Plate 145 : **No. 362 *Kidbrooke*, the final 'D' Class tank to be built, stands at Hove with a line of dumb-buffered Stephenson Clarke wagons c1902. That company held the locomotive coal contract for the LB&SCR and their wagons were much in evidence. In the carriage sidings is a rake of Stroudley six-wheel Firsts of diagram 37/44. The board seen under the footbridge advertises the firm of Horace Saunders, formerly James Ireland & Co., Timber Merchant, whose office and Central Yard here was linked to the Brighton Saw Mill in Church Street. Immediately above the locomotive are the offices of the South of England Dairies Ltd, since demolished.**

Plate 146 : **Now in Bennett home territory, this beautiful portrait of 'G' Class Single No. 335 *Connaught* taken from Henry Bennett's favourite location at the east end of the westbound platform, made for a classic picture, ideal in the late morning light for photographing trains heading east. The picture was taken when the class were still in command of the services out of Portsmouth (note the old P shed code before it became FRAT in 1903) before the 'B2's replaced them.**
courtesy Lawrence Marshall collection

Plate 147 : **Another prime Hove portrait depicting 'Gladstone' No. 189 *Edward Blount* with its notable ascription 'Gold Medal Paris Exhibition 1889'. Built in July that year, it was the first of the class to enter traffic with cast-steel coupled wheels and crescent shaped balance weights. Indirectly it was the cause of its designer's untimely end, taking part in trials between Paris and Laroche, in the course of which Stroudley caught a chill and bronchitis from which he died. It is seen here fitted in 1908 with Hammond's patent apparatus for directing pre-heated air to the firebox. (For details see page 64).**

courtesy Lawrence Marshall collection

Plate 148 : **At this choice Bennett location 'D3' No. 365 *Victoria* waits to leave Hove on the last leg of its journey to Brighton, its home shed. At one point it was the charge of John Whittle (alias 'Hellfire Jack'), who resided at Brighton during his entire career in the service of the LB&SCR. His early driving was done in France, he passed his test drive before Stroudley in 1875 and died in 1913 soon after taking part in the trial tests of Lawson Billinton's 'K' Class 2-6-0s. The driver in the cab is more likely to be George White who had charge of No. 365 from November 1904. Withdrawn in December 1952, it held the record for the class of 1,760,235 miles.**

Plate 149 : **Standing at Hove with its distinctive oast-house like building behind the footplate, No. 41, the last of the batch of Marsh's five 'H1' Class Atlantics, which appeared in February 1906, cuts a majestic pose added to by the self consciousness of the neatly dressed engine crew. The driver is John Tompsett of Brighton Shed.**

Plate 150 : **During the crisis caused by the re-organisation of Brighton Works under Marsh, which caused a vast backlog of engines awaiting repairs and a consequent shortage in the stock of working locomotives, 'E4' Class No. 512 (formerly *Kingswood*) was among several 'E4's pressed into service straight from overhaul and as yet unpainted in Marsh umber, running in a lead undercoat in August 1905. At this point it was transferred from Littlehampton Shed to Brighton and was later spare engine. Its driver was Harry Mitchell.**

Plate 151 : **An unidentified 'Gladstone' stands at the eastern end of Hove, receiving attention from an engineman at the front end. The date is the mid-1890s when sleepers were covered with ballast. Interesting features include (from left to right) the little white cabin, gas lamp, the East signal box (later Hove A) and, not least, the tall bracketed signal post at the platform end with its four square frame. To the right of the locomotive is a decorative classical chimney probably used in connection with the heating plant at a nursery shown on an 1890s Ordnance Survey map. The line of housing hints at early urbanisation, and on the extreme right next to the loading bay stands a furniture pantechnicon belonging to Taylor's Depository which was at Elephant & Castle, London.**

Plate 152 : **'Gladstone' No. 215 (formerly *Salisbury*) runs into Hove (East) on the only section of quadruple track on the Sussex coast c1908. Previously a Brighton engine, it was transferred to New Cross following overhaul in May 1906. The express from London Bridge has just come off the Cliftonville Spur, avoiding the difficult reversal at Brighton. Most of the passengers in the train would have been for destinations further along the coast.**

Plate 153 : **From this photograph one might surmise that the LB&SCR was a major player in goods traffic, but this was far from the case. E1 class No. 144 (formerly *Chambery*) of Brighton shed passes a lengthy train of empties heading back for London via the Cliftonville curve. No. 144 received the Company's initials on its side tanks in August 1906.**

Plate 154 : **Photographs taken on the Cliftonville Spur line (avoiding Brighton) are rare indeed. Ralph Stent remembers this moment well: *'This was a Saturday about 12.30pm in 1903, coming down the spur to go to Hove, then to Brighton yard, because the Brighton main line was too busy to let 'D' tank No. 297* Bonchurch*, the Paint Shop pilot, cross over the main line'.* The signal post was taken out in 1932 at the time of the Brighton electrification.**

Plate 155 : **Billinton 'D3' No. 384 *Cooksbridge* on a special treat return working from the coast is seen in the vicinity of Holland Road Halt as it heads back to Brighton, its home depot. It was to soldier on until 1909 before losing its Stroudley livery. Built in December 1893 and lasting until October 1953 as the last surviving 'D3', it topped up the second highest mileage of the class with 1,643,311 to its credit.**

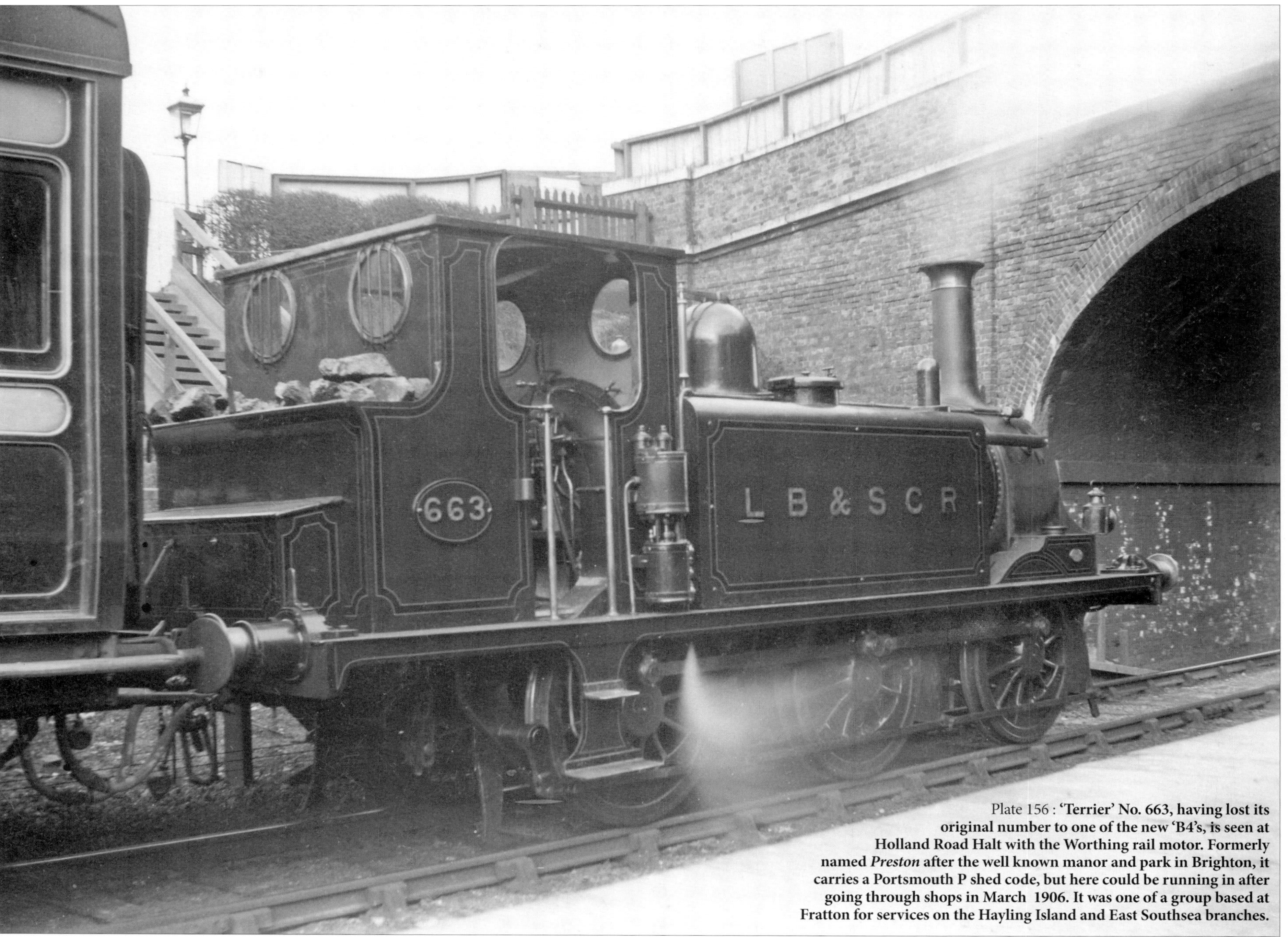

Plate 156 : **'Terrier' No. 663, having lost its original number to one of the new 'B4's, is seen at Holland Road Halt with the Worthing rail motor. Formerly named *Preston* after the well known manor and park in Brighton, it carries a Portsmouth P shed code, but here could be running in after going through shops in March 1906. It was one of a group based at Fratton for services on the Hayling Island and East Southsea branches.**

Plate 157 : **Sequentially this view should be between the two on the opposite page but is too good not to include full page. The 'Terrier' responsible for the branch service to Kemp Town (quite often No. 64 *Kemptown* itself, though strangely spelt in different fashion to the Brighton suburb), runs round its train at Brighton before returning with another working of the frequent tram-competitive service. On the left is a glimpse of Brighton's West and South signal boxes and to the right is the pleasant flowery approach to the works entrance. The notice on the signal post warns persons crossing the boards seen at the right lower corner regarding illegal entry to the works, but the uniformed person leaving the entrance has chosen to go up the platform end for convenience. The route indicator B denotes the use (from the east) of five reversible running lines, while the cylinder hanging from the pole is a self adjusting arc light known as a Jablashkoff candle.**

Plate 158 : **From Walter Bennett's caption on reverse – his Ls are written like 7s – this is supposed to be the trial trip as a 2-4-0T taken near Holland Road, and held, according to Bradley from 3rd-11th June 1905, but lacks the double diamond headcode which, as it stands, is the one allotted to the Brighton-Worthing rail motor. Around 1895 No. 82 *Boxhill* had moved to Bognor and was later sub-shedded at Midhurst before being selected by Marsh with No. 81 for conversion. It ran in Stroudley goods green unlike its companion painted in umber. It was returned to six-coupled in June 1913.**

Plate 159 : **The coast line out of Brighton veered from the London main line at Montpelier Junction before crossing the ten million brick London Road viaduct and reaching the first station at London Road, just short of which were a set of carriage sidings. No. 673 (formerly *Deptford*) is seen there on the Kemp Town motor train service. When acquiring its number in the 6xx series, it received transfer numerals and then wooden number plates (see photograph, page 111) and went through shops in July 1906 and again early in 1912 for reboilering to class 'A1x'. However, after some service on the Longmoor Military Railway c1916, it was sold in April 1919 to the Edge Hill Light Railway. This closed in 1925 but EHLR No. 1 was not scrapped till 1946, being cut up on site.**

Plate 160 : **'Terrier' No. 63 *Preston* reverses in the course of running round its train. Passengers are making their way towards the exit as the points are changed. Kemp Town was not unlike a model railway layout, the tracks plunging straight out of the station into a lengthy single bore tunnel set in the chalk cliff in the background. Note the diminutive signal cabin to the left of the tunnel mouth, the horse cart traffic in the yard before the advent of motor transport and the close-coupled carriage set used prior to the arrival of the motor train services. *Preston*, as one would expect, was a Brighton based engine in its earlier days and the neat picture with covered sleepers an early Bennett of the late 1890s.**

Plate 161 : **A fine study of No. 81 at Kemp Town as a 2-4-0T in Marsh umber. From 1906 a half-hourly rail motor service was introduced to counter competition from electric tramcars. Chances of success were greatly reduced by wartime closure between 1st January 1917 and 10th August 1919, during which the passenger traffic transferred to the roads, never to return to the railway. Passenger services ceased on 1st January 1933, but Brighton East Goods Depot remained open until 14th August 1971, relieving the cramped conditions at the main Brighton goods depot.**

Plate 162 : **In the chalky arena that was Kemp Town Station and yards, 'E3' Class radial tank No. 167 *Saddlescombe* of Brighton Shed makes up a goods train for its return to Brighton Lower Goods Yard. Kemp Town was a residential suburb east of Brighton to which the $1^1/_4$ mile branch was opened on 2nd August 1869 in response to a Beckenham, Lewes & Brighton scheme of 1863 backed by both the Chatham and South Eastern companies.**

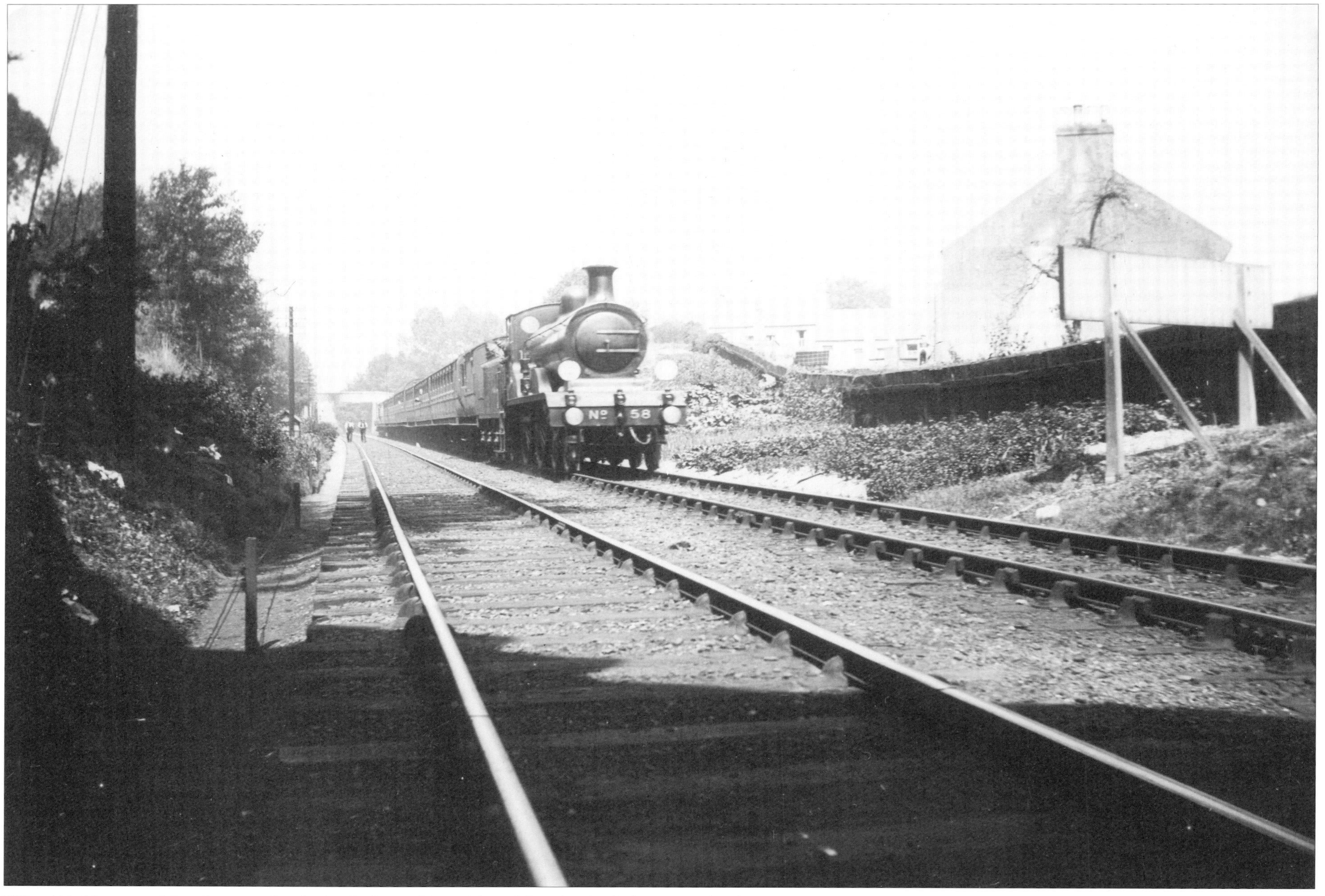

TPlate 163 : **his enterprising shot was taken in the shadows of Lewes Tunnel (West) as 'B4' Class No. 58 heads a Hastings working through Lewes. The photograph is 1909 or later as No. 58 then named *Kitchener* went through works that year. The signboard on the right is intriguing but, comparing it with similar boards in other photographs, it must be a WHISTLE sign to warn any permanent way staff that might be inside the tunnel.**

Plate 164 : **The unique larger boilered 'B3' Class engine No. 213 *Bessemer* was converted to Class 'B2x' in November 1908, as were all the 'B2's at various other dates. No. 213 was allowed to retain its name, that of the famous steel processing family, the back garden of whose mansion had a footpath directly on to the Up platform at Newick & Chailey Station where Madge Bessemer fought a courageous rearguard action to keep the Lewes-East Grinstead line open. It is seen here emerging with the Continental Express from the south portal of Lewes Tunnel (West).**

Plate 165 : **At the same location at the Lewes Station end of the tunnel and again taken from ground level, with the Southover Road bridge behind the photographer (see picture opposite), Class 'C2' No. 550, which entered traffic in January 1902, emerges with a goods special. Note the signal on the right on the impressive gantry lowered for the Lewes goods avoiding line which veered off to the right a few yards farther on. The headcode indicates a train from Willow Walk (Bricklayers Arms) to Newhaven, Eastbourne or Hastings, but could be used for starting points elsewhere in London i.e. Lillie Bridge.**

Plate 166 : **As seen in the previous picture, there was a walk inside the railings for the signalman to attend to the lamps on the gantry, but the photographer has stood himself slightly up the grass bank to obtain this delightful shot of 'Gladstone' No. 192 emerging on the Continental Express with the London Bridge portion via the Quarry Line bound for Newhaven. The former *Jacomb Hood* was a Battersea engine which had gone through works in the spring of 1907.**

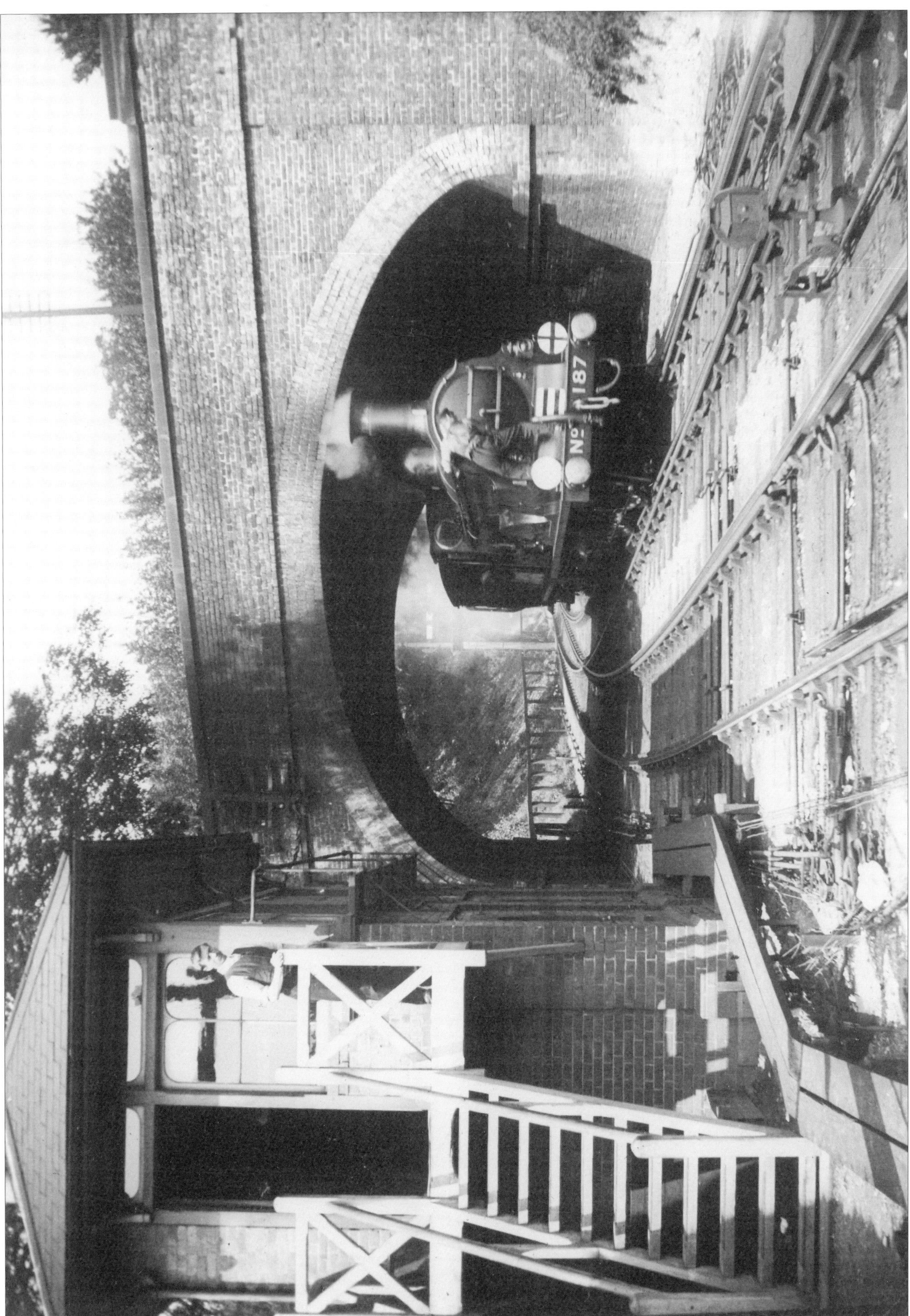

Plate 167 : **A little further on another 'Gladstone' 'B1' No. 187 (formerly *Philip Rose*, named after the Company's solicitor and later a knighted director), receives some attention up front underneath the Southover Road bridge as it passes the Lewes West box of 1888 where signalman Ager stands on duty. The photograph is taken from the north-west end of the Up London platform.**

Plate 168 : **A wonderfully clear stationscape showing the 1889 rebuilt layout at Lewes Station. The original curve, which became the goods avoiding lines is seen diverging to the left. The view is taken looking south-west from the road bridge seen in the previous picture. In the Up London platform 'B4' No. 42 *His Majesty* awaits the right away in 1909 with a London express. It went through shops in the spring of 1905 just as Marsh arrived at Brighton and so retained its Stroudley livery. The train is returning from Hastings where No. 42 was based at St. Leonards Shed in the care of driver Harry Good.**

Plate 169 : **A pleasant portrait of pioneer Stroudley 'D2' Class No. 300 *Lyons*, which gave its name to the class of fourteen 0-4-2s. It is seen here on humble duties at Lewes, humble for a locomotive that in its heyday was responsible for working the Grande Vitesse vans between London and Newhaven. A Brighton based engine, it regularly worked the 7.50am to London Bridge and then took the 2.10pm Down to Hastings before returning to Brighton over the coast road. Its final days were eked out at Tunbridge Wells and it was finally broken up in June 1903.**

Plate 170 : **Billinton 'E5' Class radial 0-6-2T No. 594 pauses for attention and refreshment in the eastbound platform on the Brighton side at Lewes. The London line platforms can be glimpsed in the right background. No. 594 *Shortbridge* was a New Cross engine under driver Rowland Reed from the day of entering traffic on 20th April 1904.**

Plate 171 : ***Goodwood*** **was a 'Belgravia' Class 2-4-0. The newly installed William Stroudley had inherited six sets of heavy iron plates ordered by his predecessor, John Chester Craven, from the Avonside Engine Company, and four sets were used for the initial quartet of double framed 'B' Class 2-4-0s completed in 1872. It is numbered here as 502, making this a pre-1899 photograph, for in that October it was again renumbered to 602. Bradley relates how this engine failed near Lewes on 15th December 1895 and remained in store for over three years, then remarkably received a new copper firebox and set of brass tubes in March 1898 and soldiered on until January 1902. The location of this photograph is uncertain, though probably at Lewes, but the veteran, based at Brighton with a train of Stroudley 4- and 6-wheel carriages is seen here a few years before withdrawal.**

Plate 172 : **'D' Class tank No. 272 *Goring* stands by the water crane at the eastern end of the Down platform from London at Lewes. It had started life in May 1880 as *Nevill* but this was changed to *Goring* in July 1897, the former name being conferred on the oddly numbered Class 'B2' No. 171. No. 272 was a Tunbridge Wells engine at this time, and received Marsh umber livery in August 1908.**

Plate 173 : **The 'I4' Class was another less than successful Marsh 4-4-2T design, being a superheated version of his 'I2' Atlantic tanks. With the backcloth of the South Downs near Lewes, No. 33 hauls an Eastbourne excursion which has come down from London via the recently opened Quarry line and is heading towards the crossing over the River Ouse and Southerham Junction, where the line to Newhaven branched off. A ganger admires Marsh's latest creation, and is seen again in the next picture, showing that the two photographs were taken on the same day.**

Plate 174 : **In February 1909 'E4' Class No. 466 not only lost its former name *Honor Oak* but underwent a rebuild, acquiring a Marsh 'I2' Class boiler and, among other additions, a smoke box door of the protruding dished variety. Not long after on 7th April that year Henry Bennett photographed it at Southerham, named after a nearby farm. Though the signal is off for Polegate, the 'E4x' has come to a halt near the point where the line crosses the Ouse, the driver seizing the opportunity to exchange words with the same ganger who is standing in front of one of Corrall's coal wagons. The train contains three heavily lime-coated cattle trucks, a prevalent hygienic practice at this time.**

Plate 175 : **A welcome pause in shunting for the crew of 'Terrier' No. 76 *Hailsham* at Polegate, and a novel use for the Stroudley tool box. For the first part of its career this locally named locomotive was stationed at the town of that name, engaged in working the branch trains to Polegate, but was transferred to Eastbourne in the early 1880s. It was sadly one of the early 'Terrier' demises, being broken up in June 1903 following withdrawal that January.**

Plate 176 : **Robert Billinton 'D3' Class 0-4-4T No. 368 *Newport* stands with a local set of coaches in Polegate West Yard with a substantial three-storey private warehouse, also seen on the right in the previous picture, behind the locomotive. This is probably the grain warehouse of Rubie & Adams Ltd, corn importers with the top of its impressive sack hoist discernible above the engine's cab. No. 368 is far from its home base at New Cross but has just come down on a special excursion, stabled at Polegate until the return working. The photograph is pre-August 1906.**

Plate 177 : **Polegate station from the west with a 'B2' which has just taken water from the crane on the Up main platform with a 'D' Class tank on a local in the loop. The signals are those installed when the station was resited in 1881, and offer an excellent guide to LB&SCR practice of the period. The chimneys and roof of the Italianate station building are visible on the left and survives today as an up-market hostelry.**

Plate 178 : **A 'Gladstone' runs into Polegate with a train from Eastbourne and, judging by the covered ballast, the date could be around 1898. The timber East box of 1881 is on the right. The wagons on the left include three Open As together with a number of private owner wagons, the nearest belonging to Clifton Collieries. The reverse tells us the engine is No. 185 *George A. Wallis* of Eastbourne Shed.**

Plate 179 : **Henry Bennett may well have known a fellow photographer, A. H. Fellows and purchased some of the latter's prints, and even been inspired to visit the latter's favourite spot by the Pevensey Levels where sheep were grazed in the summer months before being taken to other more sheltered parts of Sussex. This photograph is not a deep sepia print and shows local favourite 'E4' No. 469 *Beachy Head* trundling a short train of coal trucks, in all probability bound for Eastbourne Shed via the west side of the Stone Cross triangle between Polegate and Hampden Park.**

Plate 180 : **As mentioned in the introduction, purveyors of LB&SCR photographs were not averse to acquiring prints of other, often earlier, Brighton cameramen to enhance their own collections. This picture is of 'Gladstone' No. 219 *Cleveland* hauling an Eastbourne bound express from London past the Pevensey Levels was taken by A. H. Fellows although it appears in the Bennett collection.**

Plate 181 : **Just a few hundred yards on, this delightful portrait of the pioneer 'D3' Class 0-4-4T, which emerged named *Goldsmid* in June 1892, came to prominence by appearing on every LB&SCR engineman's cap badge. It was renamed *Havant* in September 1895, conceding its name to a new 'B2' Class No. 316. The Brighton based locomotive is in charge of a local service, probably the shuttle which ran from Hailsham through Polegate to Eastbourne.**

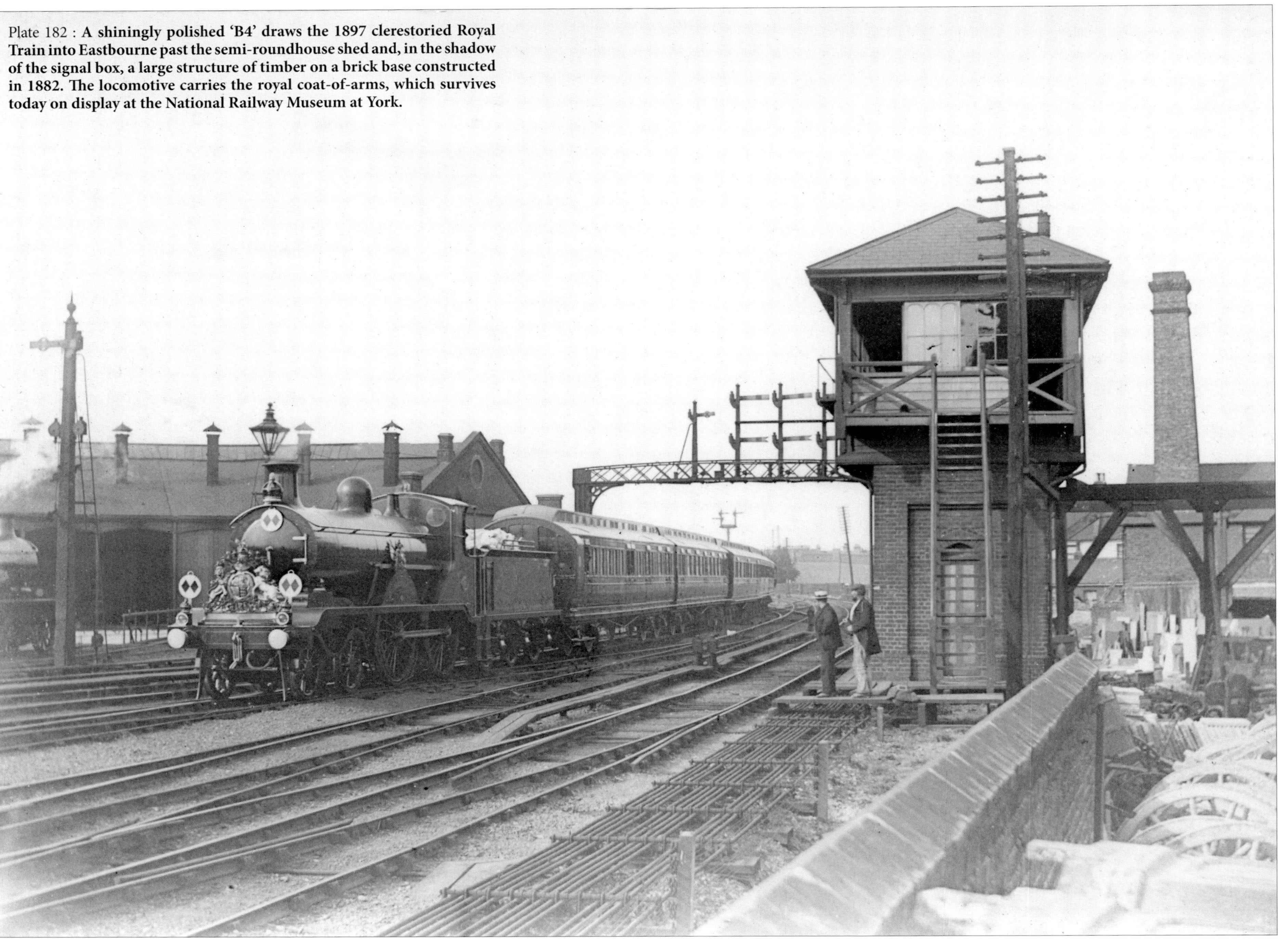

Plate 182 : **A shiningly polished 'B4' draws the 1897 clerestoried Royal Train into Eastbourne past the semi-roundhouse shed and, in the shadow of the signal box, a large structure of timber on a brick base constructed in 1882. The locomotive carries the royal coat-of-arms, which survives today on display at the National Railway Museum at York.**

Plate 183 : **The proportions of an 'E4' and the final development of the Robert Billinton radial tank, the 'E6' Class, can be compared in this view of the yard outside old Eastbourne Shed. The 'E4' is No. 497 *Donnington* and the 'E6', whose name is almost indistinguishable, is No. 409 *Graffham*, which after initial out of town postings at Horsham and Littlehampton came to Eastbourne. No. 497 was a Brighton based engine.**

Plate 184 : **A second and more close up glimpse ahead of the loco yard at Eastbourne's roundhouse, as 'B4' No. 58 *Kitchener* pauses before moving down to its waiting train at Eastbourne Station. The right-hand part of this photograph provides a rare glance of the shed precincts including the foreman's hut and of locomotives coaling up, mainly 'D' Class tanks and a 'D3', whereas most photographers would have gone for the standard turntable shot in front of the semi-roundhouse.**

Plate 185 : **A fine portrait of 'Richmond' Class 0-4-2 No. 511 *Cavendish*, an Eastbourne engine if ever there was one, for the Dukes of Devonshire owned most of the land in the town. The engine started as No. 211 *Beaconsfield*, lost it to a 'Gladstone' in November 1885, becoming *Cavendish* and in October 1897 No. 511. It then became No. 611 in the Duplicate series in June 1901 and was broken up exactly two years later. It stands on home ground at the entrance to the goods yard with the end wall of the roundhouse style engine shed beyond. Other attractive features include the local coal merchant's plot (left) and other antiquated buildings (right). Also in the area behind the locomotive the 1910 OS map shows two laundries and a nursery.**

Plate 186 : **'G' Class Single No. 349 *Albany* was a Battersea locomotive belonging to an earlier generation than the 'Gladstones'. The engine is considerably less ornate and florid than its later counterpart in the next picture. It stands ready to take empty stock out of Eastbourne terminus with the landmark of the conical tower bearing the words Eastbourne Electric Light Works .**

Plate 187 : **In John Minnis' words: '*Decoration of locomotives for the excursions from London to Eastbourne in aid of the Station Masters and Inspectors Mutual Aid and Widows Fund, became an art form. Rivalry between Battersea and New Cross sheds, who prepared the engines for the Victoria and London Bridge trains respectively, was intense*'. 'Gladstone' Class No. 217 *Northcote*, a New Cross engine, displays its finery on the turntable outside the shed.**

Plate 188 : **One usually associates the Station Masters and Inspectors excursions from London with tender locomotives. Certainly it was usual to select one of the newest, still immaculate, locomotives for these duties. Here 'D3' Class No. 376 *Folkington*, a New Cross engine which had been allocated new to that shed in March 1895, stands on the turntable at Eastbourne, quite probably in that same year.**

Plate 189 : **Stroudley 'Gladstone' Class No. 217 *Northcote* again, standing at Eastbourne with the familiar oast house landmark in view behind the tender, coupled to a set of Pullman coaches. When in 1907 the Pullman Car Company proposed to build a new entirely British built train supplanting the Pullman Limited, the famous Southern Belle inaugurated on 1st November 1908, the former stock was transferred to the Eastbourne service, seen here. *Northcote* appears to have completed the shunting of the now empty set in the middle road between the platform lines.**

Plate 190 : **The apparatus in the background of this sharp photograph of 'B2' No. 203 *Henry Fletcher*, which is decorated for an excursion, is part of the equipment of the Eastbourne Electric Light Company at their works in Junction Road, providing illumination to town and seafront. In 1900 the Eastbourne Corporation acquired the Company and moved it to another site. The premises became Messrs Beeney's Corn Store, until destroyed by enemy action in 1943.**

Plate 191 : **Henry Bennett was always on the lookout for a photograph with a good selling point – 'Gladstone' No. 183 *Eastbourne* at its namesake town. This should not have been too difficult to achieve since the engine was allocated to the shed of the same name! The picture was taken prior to the summer of 1906, for No. 183 was an early candidate for assuming Marsh umber livery, which it did that September.**

Plate 192 : **Preparing to leave. 'B4' Class No. 63** ***Pretoria*** **of Eastbourne Shed is made ready for the demanding run to London. Driver William Miller, oil can in hand poses standing on the running plate while his fireman moves coal forward to shorten the carry of his shovel. The engine's name was removed in August 1907. On the far right is Bradfords No. 2 coal wharf.**

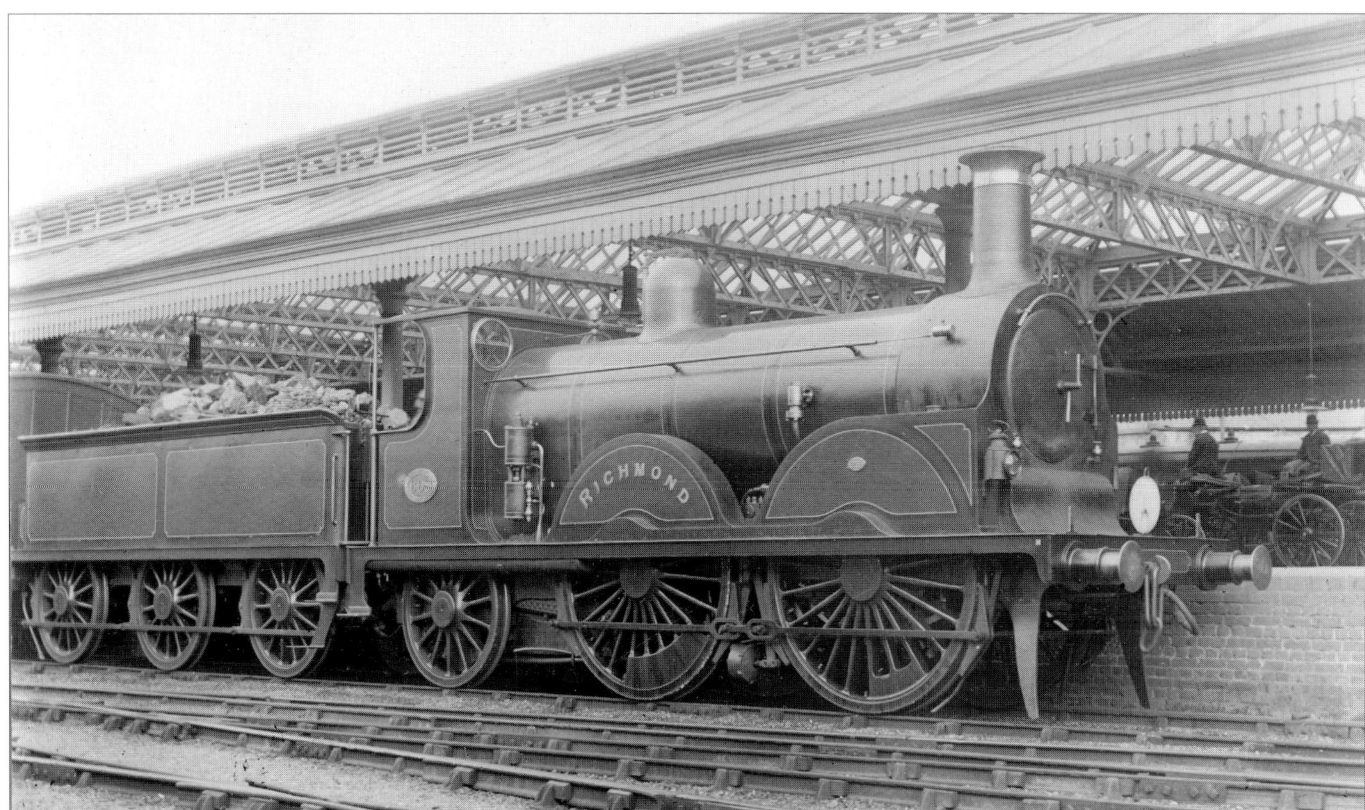

Plate 193 : **No. 608 *Richmond*, which gave its name to the small class of six engines, is seen at Eastbourne between 1897 and 1903 when it was withdrawn. The class formed the antecedent of the celebrated 'Gladstones', a transitional phase in Stroudley's quest for a standard express engine. In the 'Gladstones' he did away with iron frames and outside framed tenders, widened the footplate and introduced steam lubrication and new braking arrangements. A glimpse of the fine roof spanning the cab road, added in 1898, illustrates the grand scale on which the station was rebuilt in 1886, befitting this jewel of the south coast.**

Plate 194 : **Although a Brighton based locomotive, Stroudley 'E1' Class 0-6-0T No. 136 *Brindisi* has been all the way along the east coast line to Hastings where it is seen in the shadow of the SER's engine shed, ready to take a return goods westwards. The LB&SCR and SER companies came into hot conflict in their desire to secure the Hastings business in 1851. Eventually receipts were shared.**

Plate 195 : **Henry Bennett took this much published portrait of 'Terrier' No. 46 *Newington* at Kensington (Addison Road), seen here operating a shuttle service which survived right through to the end of steam in 1967. The LB&SCR owned a one-sixth share in the West London Extension Company with running powers throughout. *Newington* was sold in 1903 to the L&SWR and on in 1913 to the Freshwater, Yarmouth & Newport Railway. It returned to the mainland in 1949 and on withdrawal was purchased by the Sadler Rail Coach Co. at Droxford on the West Meon line, then sold on to Brickwoods for display outside The Hayling Billy pub; it finally returned to the island to continue its adventurous career on the Isle of Wight Steam Railway in 1979.**

Plate 196 : **Stroudley 'Terrier' No. 36 *Bramley* is photographed at Wimbledon, having come up on the local service from West Croydon, its home shed. Its driver at the turn of the century was George Pavey. This is an early Bennett photograph, for in 1902 it was sold for £670 together with four others of the class to Pauling & Co., the contractors constructing the Northolt-High Wycombe extension of the new Great Central Railway. It was fitted with dumb buffers and tyre washing pipes, and had the guard irons removed, becoming the contractor's No. 88.**

Plate 197 : **Yet another outlying 'Terrier' No. 77 *Wonersh* has its smoke box cleared out as it stands outside Midhurst Shed, where the engine was based almost continually from the time it left New Cross in 1883 till its transfer to Littlehampton in 1900. The original timber shed was lengthened but became so tumbledown that it was replaced by a new shed in 1907, again in wood, on the same site.**

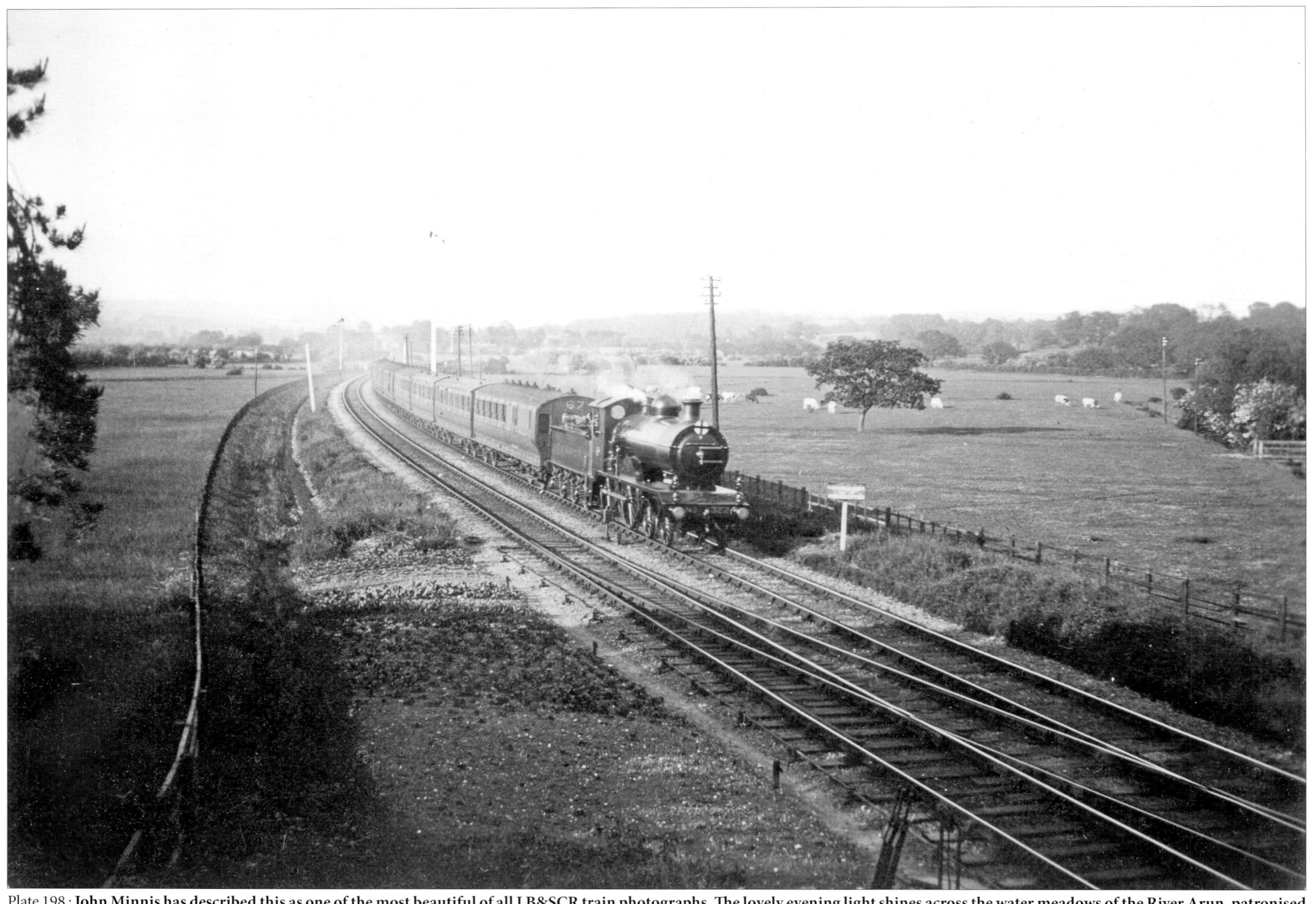

Plate 198 : **John Minnis has described this as one of the most beautiful of all LB&SCR train photographs. The lovely evening light shines across the water meadows of the River Arun, patronised by a herd of largely all-white cows. The locomotive is 'B2x' Class 4-4-0 No. 322 (formerly *G. P. Bidder*), which lost its name when rebuilt in 1908, hauls a Portsmouth-bound fast comprising bogie stock and is seen approaching Arundel from the north.**

Plates 199, 200 & 201 : **Henry Bennett was quick to get photographs on sale of one of the most dramatic accidents of the time. 'D' Class tank No. 297 *Bonchurch* while working the 8.18am Eastbourne to Tunbridge Wells train down Tooth's Bank between Heathfield and Mayfield on 1st September 1897, left the rails and keeled over while some of the carriages came to rest at the foot of a steep embankment. Remarkably Driver James McKenly was the only fatal casualty, though there were several injuries in the wrecked coaches. It must be left open as to whether Bennett got to the scene of the accident or whether he obtained the photographs from someone who did, but the originals are reproduced in his distinctive sepia format.**

Plate 202 : **A number of 'G' Class Singles eked out their final days operating from Tunbridge Wells Shed. Bennett was extra keen to photograph No. 342 *St Lawrence*, which was posted to that shed from 18th January 1905, the driver being Walter Reeves, that the full array of locomotives on shed was missed out on this occasion. However, 'E1' No. 128 *Avignon*, the spare goods engine and shunter appears on the extreme left, and behind stands 'D' Class No. 351 *Chailey*, both shed residents.**

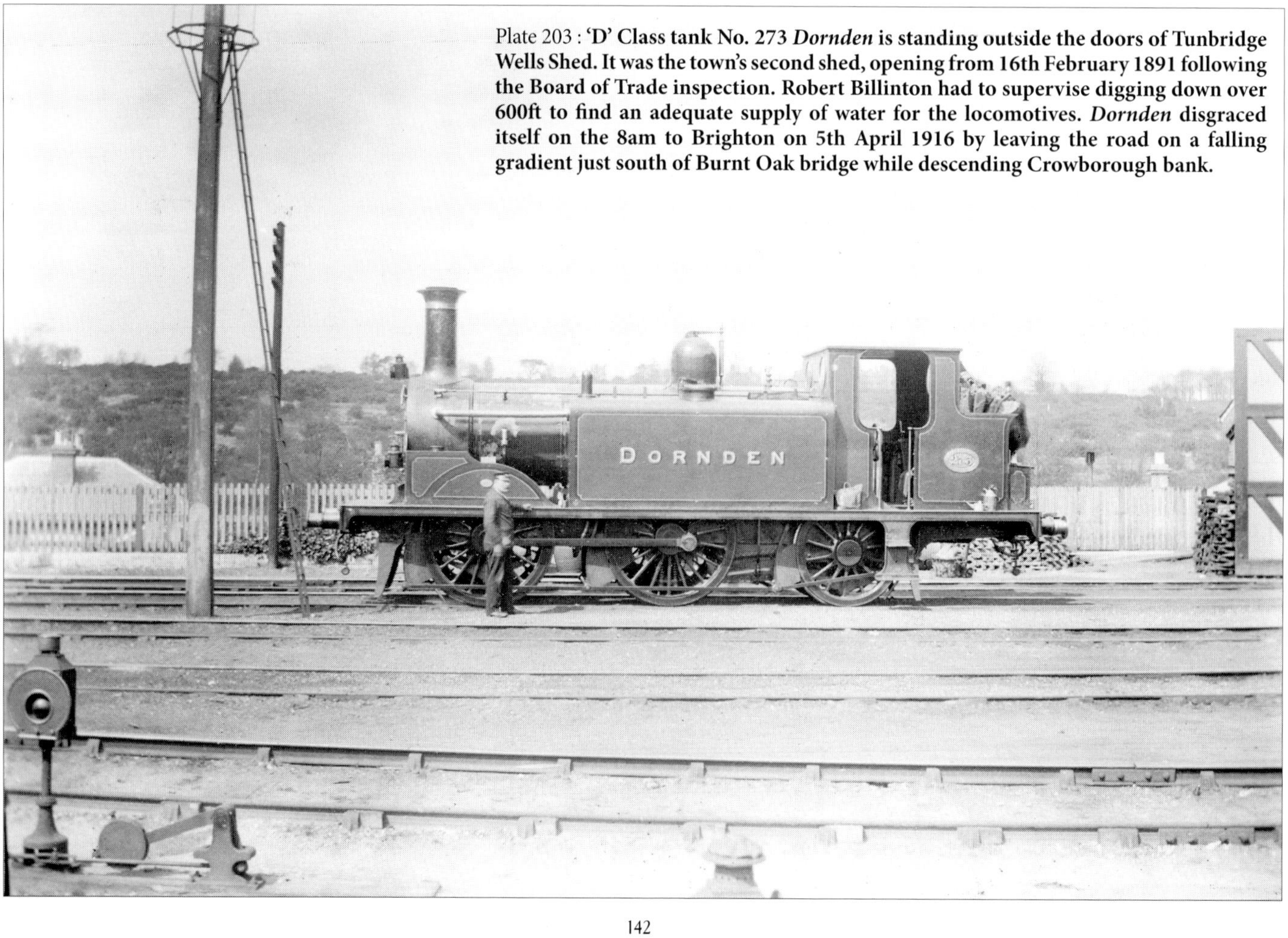

Plate 203 : **'D' Class tank No. 273 *Dornden* is standing outside the doors of Tunbridge Wells Shed. It was the town's second shed, opening from 16th February 1891 following the Board of Trade inspection. Robert Billinton had to supervise digging down over 600ft to find an adequate supply of water for the locomotives. *Dornden* disgraced itself on the 8am to Brighton on 5th April 1916 by leaving the road on a falling gradient just south of Burnt Oak bridge while descending Crowborough bank.**

Plate 204 : **Ralph Stent has no recollection of ever visiting the west siding at East Grinstead, adjacent to the line to Three Bridges. The musketeers would have been too young for that. The single siding was used to store locomotives awaiting sale or scrapping. The majority of pictures taken here were by the Chambers brothers, but this one of 'D' Class tank No. 8 *Brockley* appears in the Bennett collection. It was withdrawn in April 1904 and finally broken up that July.**

Plate 205 : **Another early Victorian photograph in the collection taken in the mid-1890s, when ballast was still used to cover the sleepers, has captured Stroudley 'C' Class 0-6-0 No. 415, known as the 'Kitson Goods' after the company that built them, seen at the head of a northbound goods passing the signalman on duty in the South Box at East Grinstead (Low Level).**

Plate 206 : **We conclude where we began, at Horsted Keynes where 'E4' Class radial No. 562 *Laughton* stands by the signal box c1906. Next to it on the right is one of the half-dozen Stroudley 'C1' Class goods 0-6-0s also stored there. No. 562 survived the long queue for Brighton works, eventually being restored to traffic in 1909 when it lost its name. Here it is still in Stroudley livery, carrying its original boiler with the lock up safety valves. It was later given a boiler with Salter safety valves and saw service with the Railway Operating Division in France 1918-19, and soldiered on until withdrawn in August 1960.**

Plate 207 : **Bennett's much published classic masterpiece of the locomotives stored at Horsted Keynes from 1905-1909 whilst Brighton works was being rebuilt and extended under Marsh. Prominent by the signal box (which still stands today on the Bluebell Railway as a listed building) is 'E Special' (later Class 'E3') No. 158 *West Brighton*, Stroudley's posthumous 0-6-2T completed by his successor, Robert Billinton. A count of twenty-nine chimneys shows the extent of the locomotives which included representatives of classes 'B4', 'C1', 'D', 'D2', 'E1', 'E3', 'E4' and 'E5'. Taken from the top of the water tower, it affords a view across to the station with its complete set of canopies, and tall topiary bushes on each platform.**